D1306557

EMPLOYED Mother HOOD

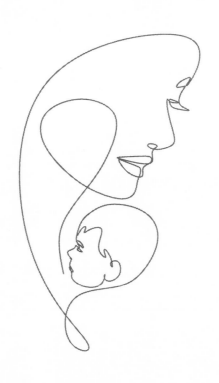

EMPLOYED MOTHERHOOD

Healthily and Holistically Transition Back to Work After Having a Baby

Becky Morrison Gleed LMFT PMH-C

First published by Becky Morrison Gleed

Copyright © 2023

All rights reserved. No part of this book may be reproduced, stored in a retrieval system, communicated or transmitted, in any form or by any means without prior written approval. All inquiries should be made to the publisher.

Employed Motherhood: Healthily and Holistically Transition Back to Work After Having a Baby is intended as a self-guide. It is not intended to replace psychiatric and/or medical treatment for disorders diagnosed in the perinatal period. While best efforts have been made to prepare this book with evidence-based information, the author and publisher make no representations of any kind and assume no liabilities. Further, they shall not be held liable or responsible to any person or entity for having caused harm, directly or indirectly. Each woman's perinatal experience is unique and therefore, this book may not be suitable for all. It is recommended that you consult with and seek out the help of a licensed professional should you need treatment.

Dedicated to all of the Women who came before and paved the way to make employed motherhood possible.

"I can do things you cannot. you can do things I cannot: together we can do great things."

~ Mother Teresa

CONTENTS

CHAPTER 1

CHAPTER 2

CHAPTER 3

INTELLECTUAL WELLNESS...............................79

CHAPTER 4

PHYSICAL WELLNESS 92

CHAPTER 5

ENVIRONMENTAL WELLNESS........................115

CHAPTER 8

PREFACE

TO THE SECOND EDITION

In early March 2020, my family took a long-awaited trip to Portugal. To prepare to take two young kids across the Atlantic, I stopped at the pharmacy to grab a few supplies. As I chatted with the pharmacist about our upcoming international adventure, she slid a small box of medical grade masks across the counter. "You're going to want these," she said. I thanked her, made the $2.99 purchase, and went home to pack our bags.

Like all of us who lived through this unprecedented time, I have a seemingly infinite number of stories from those early pandemic days that confirm the unusual flavors of early pandemic life, as we sprinted (sometimes in the wrong direction) alongside scientific discovery to keep ahead of the ever-changing tsunami of news. Like meeting with a patient in March 2020 (unmasked!) and then strategizing at length about how to handle her $20 cash copay so that no COVID would pass between us (we decided to set it down on the sofa and spray it with Lysol). Or figuring out how to use telehealth and realizing that the stone tiles of our New Mexico home created a perfect echo chamber for my daughter's screams – and not the perfect soundtrack for my clients.

Unlike the 3.5 million mothers who left the workforce in March -April 2020, I was fortunate enough to be able to continue my work as a Licensed Marriage and Family Therapist during this time, and to do so remotely.[1] This made it possible for me to have a direct insight into the experience of how women in the perinatal period were living through this seismic shift. I saw women grapple with being forced to go to their medical appointments – for fertility treatments or reproductive care – without their partner or support person. Women who gave birth alone, who labored in a mask, who had to wait heartbreakingly long amounts of time to introduce their newborn to their loved ones. Pregnant women who grappled with whether to get vaccinated, without clear guidance from the government and the medical establishment. Women who suffered from postpartum depression, joining an extra large cohort – 34% of new moms versus 14% pre-pandemic.[2] Women who planned for a return-to-work that never happened, who had to renegotiate their ideas of childcare and careers and "balance," making split-second decisions to relocate, to form bubbles, to throw out their painstakingly designed Plans A, B and C and rebuild it all from scratch.

New research is coming out every day to confirm my professional observations. Sociologists, psychologists, and scholars of gender and work, conducting studies around the world, are all unearthing similar trends: Working mothers – especially younger women – were uniquely challenged by the pandemic, being forced to make impossible choices between managing their

1   Heggeness, M. L., Fields, J., García Trejo, Y. A., & Schulzetenberg, A. (2021, March 3). Tracking job losses for mothers of school-age children during a health crisis. United States Census Bureau. https://www.census.gov/library/stories/2021/03/moms-work-and-the-pandemic.html

2   Chen, Q., Li, W., Xiong, J., & Zheng, X. (2022). Prevalence and risk factors associated with postpartum depression during the COVID-19 pandemic: A literature review and meta-analysis. *International Journal of Environmental Research and Public Health, 19*(4), 1–11. https://doi.org/10.3390/ijerph19042219

home or providing for their family.[3] Some women had more flexibility than others, in terms of their ability to work from home, find safe, reliable childcare, and get support from their community. But "flexibility" isn't always a benefit when it means you are able to be pulled in twelve directions at once. One international study supports that suspicion I often heard voiced by my clients who were working from home during the pandemic shutdown phases: "For women, working from home was associated with higher prevalence of the symptoms of depression compared to traveling to a workplace."[4]

My ability to support those women – in whatever small way – pushed me to navigate and renegotiate my own working motherhood throughout the pandemic. It also inspired me to bring to completion a project I had nearly gotten across the finish line until the pandemic put it on pause: the first edition of this book, *Employed Motherhood*. As a sole practitioner in an under-resourced area, I've always wanted to extend my reach beyond what I can do one-on-one. When I first set out to research market competitors on the subject of helping new moms transition back to work, I was disappointed (but not surprised) to find so few resources – especially when you consider what a large percentage of the population goes through this experience. After readjusting to the ever-changing new "normal," I put the finishing touches on the book and put it out in the world in May 2021.

The response to the book was everything I hoped and more. The kind words I received from readers warmed my heart. The appreciation I received from fellow practitioners who were happy to be able to give this tangible piece of support to a new, struggling working mom, was absolutely priceless. The kinetic energy I felt when I sat down for interviews about the book showed me I've tapped into something bigger than me: It's a collective energy that comes from all the women who came before us and extends to future generations.

Now that the book has lived in the world for two years, it's also become apparent that the landscape for working mothers has truly changed in every possible way – and so this book has to change to reflect those shifts. Remote work brought employers, colleagues and clients into our homes, starting conversations about the invisible labor women disproportionately perform and the infinite bandwidth required to context-switch at the drop of a hat. That's not to say anything was cured; but conversations got started, and now flexible work arrangements aren't as rare as they once were.

Changes at work are just the tip of the iceberg. There have been transformations in healthcare, sea changes in our social lives, and how we relate to our environment(s). There have been political changes, too, such as the overturning of Roe v. Wade, and other restrictions on women's hard-fought rights and protections. I've made additions throughout the book to acknowledge these changes – and, at the same time, I'll be the first to say: there are 1,000s more to make and to keep making. As much as I've tried to consider all the angles and address the various kinds

---

3   Thompson, R. J. (2023). The impact of COVID-19 on working women with caring responsibilities: An interpretive phenomenological analysis. *Merits, 3*(1), 96–114. https://doi.org/10.3390/merits3010006

4   Burn, E., Tattarini, G., Williams, I., Lombi, L., & Gale, N. K. (2022). Women's experience of depressive symptoms while working from home during the COVID-19 pandemic: Evidence from an international web survey. *Frontiers in Sociology, 7*, 1–11. https://doi.org/10.3389/fsoc.2022.763088

of working motherhood, I know it's not possible to speak to every experience. Please know I've done these edits in the spirit of inclusivity, and I hope to only expand my perspectives with successive editions of the book.

If there were one major throughline to my edits, it's my greater awareness of – and hesitation towards – hustle culture. Being a new mom can feel like a juggling act. Throw in a career, additional caregiving responsibilities, and other relationships, and you've got more balls in the air than any non-circus-performer should have to handle. I work with women who have infinite commutes, who move between the C-Suite and the board of their preschool, who travel the globe, who run their own business and care for aging parents – it's hard to say to a new mom: don't try to do it all.

And, honestly, as a mental health professional, it's not up to me to tell anyone what to do. What I've aimed to do here is to acknowledge and validate the feelings that come up around the infinite hats you wear, whether out of your own choice or circumstances beyond your control; offer mindset shifts and practical advice around how to handle all those hats; and give you space to reflect on your personal values so that you're able to identify and honor what matters most to *you*.

In the past two years, something else has changed for me: I'm no longer a *new* working mother. My girls are growing up, and they're out of the all-hands-on-deck toddler phase. (Yes, it happens!) From that more seasoned perspective, I want to say that it does get easier. There will always be new challenges, but with practice, you'll get better at facing each one – until one day you look up, and there's no diaper bag in sight, just your kids playing happily in front of you.

INTRODUCTION

Conception, pregnancy, labor and delivery, motherhood, and now...employed motherhood. What other stage in life brings with it more changes than the perinatal period? None. It wouldn't be a stretch to say that early motherhood *is* transformation itself. As you navigate your new body and the unfamiliar landscape of your new hormones, alongside your ever-changing baby, new familial dynamics, societal expectations, and professional pressures, there will be unique challenges every step of the way. Among them, the transition back to work – following whatever parental leave you may have had – is no walk in the park. Quite the opposite. It is a highly emotional, stressful, and demanding experience for mothers who live in a world where we are expected to return to our pre-pregnancy bodies within six weeks, pump an abundance of breast milk, and hide a cesarean scar which is not yet fully healed – all while wearing a smile!

Years later, I vividly remember my transition back to work after my second pregnancy. It is true when they say a memory is stamped on the hippocampus with darker ink when adrenaline is involved. My emotions ran the gamut: On my first day back, I was thrilled yet overwhelmed seeing coworkers, mortified when I spilled my precious breastmilk in my supervisor's office, and alarmed that I had to *re-learn* several clinical protocols I once knew like the back of my hand. Disoriented and discouraged (to say the least), I had to acknowledge that what I was doing was not run-of-the-mill, business as usual. Adjusting my expectations was the first step toward figuring out how to move forward.

Returning to work is *hard*. I'll keep repeating that truth. It feels like a never-ending sea of compromises, less-than-perfect fixes, and on-the-spot learning. But if you shore up your support team, pack a compass and a map, and accept the fact you'll make a lot of detours, you'll find it *is* possible to be the mom and the professional you want to be–not 100% all day, every day, but enough to make the journey worth it.

This book is full of my best advice, but I know my readers: busy moms trying to hold on to any semblance of sanity. I know what you're up against, and the last thing I want to do is add to your already full plate. I offer you a lot of *do's*; they are not intended to heap more food on that plate but to suggest ways to bolster your wellness from every possible angle. Bringing all that together, if you nourish yourself fully, your actions will be more intentional and your life will settle into a new equilibrium. Yes, there will be an upfront investment, and there may not be steady, linear progress – but keep at it, and it will pay off.

I also want to honor the unique circumstances of each mother. My years of experience as a Licensed Marriage and Family Therapist have shown me there is no one-size-fits-all when it comes to employed motherhood. Each employed mother has different needs. I wrote this book by drawing on the best, most diverse resources available to me: the precious few academic papers on the subject of working motherhood (an area of research that, thanks to the pandemic, is gaining more attention), time-tested wellness principles, interviews with working moms, and my own professional and personal experience. Some of the tools I offer might be more resonant to you at certain moments. Some might not ring true to your situation. Please consider this your invitation to take what works for you, skip what doesn't, or transform the message to align more succinctly with your world. Trust your intuition.

THE LANDSCAPE OF EMPLOYED MOTHERHOOD

Why do working women leave the workforce after the birth of a child? To what extent is it a preference – and to what extent is it due to the countless constraints placed on working mothers? In order to identify tangible, concrete, supportive measures, it is vital to understand the obstacles: Are new mothers leaving – or never re-entering – the workforce because of lack of access to quality child care or employer support? Are they influenced by personal or familial factors, such as the child's temperament or health? What issues have impacted your transition back to work?

Another consideration is a woman's *preference* to work – and, if she chooses to do so, how she wants to balance her professional and personal life. A 2000 study developed by Catherine Hakim[5] categorizes women into three groups vis-à-vis the work-home dynamic: home-centered, work-centered, and adaptive. The first group, represented by 20% of women across a spectrum of educational backgrounds, prefer not to work if circumstances allow; the second group, represented by another 20%, expect to work full-time throughout life; while the third, numerically dominant group is "determined to combine employment and family work, so become[s] secondary earners. They may work full-time early in life, but later switch to part-time jobs on a semi-permanent basis, and/or to intermittent employment." Which category best represents you, and how will this knowledge serve you well as you transition back to work?

Working mothers account for nearly one-third of all employed women in the United States – 23.5 million working women have children under the age of 18, according to the US Census.[6] Now is the time for this vulnerable demographic to receive support at both micro and macro levels, particularly in the challenging period of transitioning back to work.

In order to account for the multifaceted issues that impact wellness during this transformational period, I draw from the framework as outlined by SAMHSA,[7] "the agency within the U.S. Department of Health and Human Services that leads public health efforts to advance the behavioral health of the nation."[8] I chose the SAMHSA framework because it aligns with my belief that working motherhood is not just a matter of work-home balance; it's a far more complex dynamic that encompasses every dimension of the human experience. Over the course of eight chapters, I'll explore the following dimensions of wellness:

---

5   Hakim, C. (2000). *Work-lifestyle choices in the 21st century: Preference theory.* Oxford University Press.

6   United States Department of Labor. (n.d.). *Family and Medical Leave Act.* https://www.dol.gov/agencies/whd/fmla

7   Kobrin, M. (n.d.). *Promoting wellness for better behavioral and physical health.* SAMHSA. https://mfpcc.samhsa.gov/ENewsArticles/Article12b_2017.aspx

8   Swarbrick, M. (2006). A wellness approach. *Psychiatric Rehabilitation Journal, 29*(4), 311–314. https://doi.org/10.2975/29.2006.311.314

Chapter 1, "Emotional & Psychological Wellness," starts with self-awareness, the foundational practice that makes all other positive changes possible. On top of that foundation, I'll show you how to cultivate emotional and psychological wellness by validating and affirming yourself, navigating separation anxiety, assessing expectations surrounding your many roles, mitigating mom guilt, managing stress – and knowing when everyday stress crosses into the territory of a mood disorder that requires professional help.

Chapter 2, "Spiritual Wellness," honors the call to action – the why – that draws you back to work, whatever it may be: to provide for your family, to contribute to your field, to normalize working motherhood – or some deeply personal reason. I'll discuss why it's so important to allow yourself space to nurture that "why" (even when all the practical concerns of daily life scream for our immediate attention) and give you some ideas of how to do so, through gratitude, love, and meditative prayer.

Chapter 3, "Intellectual (Cognitive) Wellness," challenges the common misconception that working motherhood runs on a constant state of low batteries and suggests cognitive benefits that go along with the challenging territory. I'll offer a range of strategies to lighten the mental load and handle the juggling act that is working motherhood, including: multitasking, listing, outsourcing.

Chapter 4, "Physical Wellness," takes a holistic approach to your ever-shifting relationship with your postpartum body, focusing on the main ingredients for healthy working motherhood. I start with the ins and outs of sleep in the perinatal period, how to maximize that precious resource, and what to do when you find yourself in short supply. I'll also talk about how to fuel your body with healthy food – putting a premium on *efficiency* in the kitchen – and offer creative suggestions for how to incorporate movement into your routine. Since our workplace wardrobe impacts physical wellness, I'll talk about ways to dress that combine comfort, efficiency, and professionalism. A chapter on physical wellness would not be complete without an in-depth look at the biggest question mark for lactating moms: pumping at work – and while traveling. The chapter concludes with a short overview of all the hormonal changes that impact your physical wellness in the perinatal period – another reason to offer yourself kindness during this transitional time.

Chapter 5, "Environmental Wellness," looks at the many environments that encircle a working mom, including the home and workplace, the neighborhood and community, and beyond. I'll give suggestions about how to tackle the challenges of maintaining an organized and clean (but not *sparkling* clean) home, office, and car in order to help you feel more relaxed, creative, and in control. I'll also discuss ways to get involved with your community by taking advantage of local resources and contributing to meaningful causes. Then, looking at the broader environment, I'll talk about how to find support, engage in activism (when you have the time and energy!), and make small but significant changes to help Mother Earth.

Chapter 6, "Financial Wellness," helps you make the trek through the economic challenges that often accompany working motherhood by taking a twofold approach: on the one hand, I give you concrete resources, tools, and strategies to assess and improve your financial wellness; on the other hand, I invite you to consider how finances – and the decisions we make around spending and earning – can be impacted by our emotions. Spreadsheets, tax advisers, and regular check-ins with your partner (if you have one) are all important ingredients, but self-awareness and deep breaths are the secret sauce.

Chapter 7, "Occupational Wellness," confronts perhaps the cornerstone issue for working mothers: parental leave and how to handle the momentous return to the workplace. I'll suggest strategies for fielding inappropriate questions from coworkers without losing your cool, and I'll help you think through concrete plans for how to handle the inevitable sick day without wading through a swamp of guilt. This chapter also contains specific information about legal workplace protections and advocacy.

Last, but certainly not least, Chapter 8, "Social Wellness," embraces the multifaceted relationships you'll navigate as a working mom: with yourself, your child, your childcare provider(s), your partner, your friends and your family. These are the people who nourish us, who make us want to get out of bed every day, and…sometimes make us lose a little sleep (or a lot). Some of these relationships might be smooth sailing, while others might need some (re-)orientation. Whatever the case might be, continue to check in with yourself and use your intuition as your North Star. Putting together a team of people, in whom you trust, is an absolutely essential part of avoiding working mother burn-out – and enjoying this transitional time in your life to the fullest. In this chapter I'll also advocate the use of paid support to bolster your social wellness. No matter how caring the village you belong to, we can all benefit from the objective expertise of a trained professional, be it a doula, a physical therapist, or a counselor. Sometimes our insurance will even foot the bill – a win-win!

When thinking about the eight dimensions, you'll naturally see some overlap. That's by design, a reflection of the interrelated web of our experience. When you face an obstacle in one dimension, it will often impact the others: If you're not able to pay all your bills on time (financial), you may experience anxiety (emotional), have trouble sleeping (physical wellness), and lose interest in your hobbies (intellectual) and friendships (social). Similarly, an improvement in one area can radiate positivity into the other dimensions: If you tidy your workspace (environmental), you might feel more relaxed (emotional), increasing your work productivity (occupational) and allowing you more free time to exercise and cook (physical), hang out with friends (social), or devote to hobbies (intellectual). By breaking down the eight different dimensions, you can begin to trace a map of how the aspects of your life influence one another and develop strategies to allow wellness to spread throughout all eight.

Together, in each chapter we will walk through *how* to build your wellness in each dimension through practical strategies specifically designed for mothers transitioning to employed motherhood, many that I draw from my own experience as a full time employed mom of two young daughters. To add more voices and more perspectives to help guide you, I'll also share interviews with moms who navigated the choppy waters, laying out the map they used to find their own way. Your personal journey will be different, so pick and choose amongst the tools I lay out, to help you navigate the best path for you.

A word to mothers located outside the United States: While some aspects of the book explicitly address the American working mother's experience (especially regarding federal policies around parental leave and lactation support, workplace benefits, etc.), the research and interviews I conducted extend beyond U.S. borders. I wrote this book to reach as many working mothers as possible, regardless of geographic location; it is my hope that it will be a help to you, as well.

MY WHY

Fire burned through my bones, exuding intense heat and flames: my call to action came in my early postpartum days back at work, following the birth of my second child. My first postpartum experience had been a bumpy ride; as the first woman in my family to embrace working motherhood, I had no playbook, just abstract goals, hopes, fears – and some unhelpful voices chanting, "Daycare is bad for babies! Daycare is bad for babies!" Determined to continue making contributions to the field I love *and* to mother my baby girl with all my heart, I took a deep breath and returned to work full-time. I did not know what I was in for. Pushing through relentless fifty-hour weeks, I experienced postpartum depression and anxiety.

During my second pregnancy, knowing I was at high-risk for a recurrence and armed with the precious insight I had uncovered the first time around, I was ready for things to be different. I prepared myself as best I could, lining up every possible resource I could think of. Spoiler alert: It wasn't enough. Despite my professional training as a licensed therapist, despite my supportive partner, despite my best efforts to put together a team of mental health professionals to be there if I needed, I was under-resourced and under-supported by society. There was no way I could – or should – have done more.

During this major life transition, I found myself grasping at straws trying to find resources – let alone *helpful* ones. Discovering that the employed mothers who came before me had to function in an under-supported, under-resourced climate was nothing short of a rude awakening. *Why has this topic not grown legs and run to every media source?* When this thought runs amuck in my head, I gently remind myself that employed mothers are *tired*, not solely their bodies but their *souls*. And so, my experience lit a spark in me; I had to find a way to provide tangible support for women undergoing this major life transition.

That spark ignited into a full-fledged blaze thanks to my work in emergency psychiatric services, where I crossed paths – often in the late hours of the night – with other postpartum moms whose under-resourced, under-supported experiences brought them to a very dark place. Serving as the interface for these women and last-resort mental health services, I could see how poorly their unique needs were understood, let alone being met. Experiencing this insight at a time when I, too, was in that vulnerable, transitional, perinatal period, was nothing short of life changing.

As soon as I was able to come up for air, I set out to write this book: a genuine labor of love, researched after full days of work and mothering. The multi-dimensional research process, and the twists and turns required to put together a comprehensive resource, was a further testament to the challenges faced by working mothers. I started by turning to academic research, hiring a research assistant to help me comb through what I thought would have been voluminous quantities of material. Wishful thinking. When my assistant came to me with a paucity of academic sources, I couldn't believe my eyes – so I redid the search myself. No luck. Maybe it was our database? I contacted another researcher with access to a different database: same story. I then turned to popular books, but while many authors were happy to celebrate the contributions of women, precious few were interested in the specifics of employed mothers.

The other component of my research involved conducting interviews with working mothers to learn from their diverse experiences. My goal was to speak to women of all demographics, ages, races, life experiences, marital status, and working in different industries. I put out a call for volunteers, and word spread across my network, which brought me twenty women from different geographic regions of the United States and several other countries. As diverse as they all were, one common thread linked them all: Introverts and extroverts alike started our relationship as if walking on eggshells. They all treaded lightly, hesitant to share their stories as if they were taboo. If they had ever shared these stories at all, it was with a very select few; understandably, they all needed to test the waters, to see if it were safe to share with me. I am deeply grateful to the women who agreed to make this book one such sacred space where the intimate stories – and struggles – of working mothers can be shared without judgment.

I am here to provide representation and make our voices heard. My hope is to squash the pervasive belief that this major life transition *has to be* represented by chronic sleep deprivation, neglect of self-health, and isolation. My *why* is to send a message of hope – hope that you *can* healthily and holistically transition to employed motherhood. You do *not* have to buy in or adopt a "crash and burn" approach. Thanks to the wisdom I learned from returning to employment after two pregnancies, I can assure you that there are strategies to draw upon in each of the eight dimensions of wellness: emotional and psychological, spiritual, cognitive, physical, environmental, financial, occupational, and social. I'm looking forward to offering you guidance as you undertake this rewarding, challenging journey.

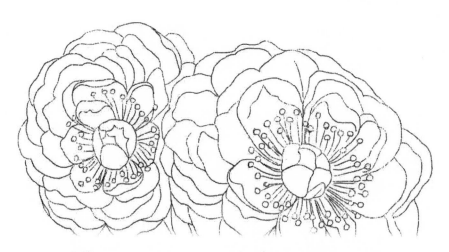

Dimension of Wellness: Emotional

NOTES

_____

_____

_____

_____

_____

_____

_____

_____

_____

_____

_____

_____

_____

_____

_____

_____

CHAPTER 1

EMOTIONAL WELLNESS

————•—∞∞∞—•————

Employed Moms' Mental Health Matters

T ransitioning back to work following the birth of a child can trigger emotions you never knew existed and magnify ones already on your radar. Tremendous postpartum change – biological, emotional, social, financial – can be enough to send any mother's already tenuous mental health into a full-blown mood disorder. Add on yet *another* strenuous and demanding transition, and survival develops an entirely new meaning.

The foundation for emotional wellness is the practice of self-awareness. Notice I call it a "practice." Self-awareness isn't a lightning bolt of inspiration that opens your eyes to the person you truly are. It takes time to get used to identifying thoughts and feelings, like building a new muscle (see Appendix A). Once you identify thoughts and feelings surrounding your return to work, turn them into an I-Feel statement that you can write in a journal, or even say out loud. It might feel silly at first, but it's great practice for sharing those thoughts and feelings with others (see Appendix B).

With a foundation of self-awareness, in this chapter, I'll teach strategies of emotional wellness by showing how to:

1. validate and empathize with your thoughts and feelings

2. affirm yourself

3. navigate separation anxiety

4. assess expectations surrounding your many roles

5. mitigate guilt

6. manage stress

7. identify when to seek professional help.

VALIDATION, BECAUSE YOU ARE WORTHY

When you hear the word "validation," what does it make you think? Validation is not just agreeing with whatever someone says but acknowledging their unique perspective and experience rather than trying to dismiss or resolve it. Validating your thoughts and feelings, as well as receiving validation from others, is more important than ever during this transition period. While one recent study revealed the immediate negative impact "invalidating feedback of emotional states ha[s]… on a person's emotional self-efficacy score,"[9] another confirmed that women were less likely to experience postpartum depression when they had family support.[10]

What does validation sound like? Have you ever said to someone, "I'm so scared I'm going to mess up the presentation," and they reply, "Don't worry, you always say that, and then it goes great!"? That's a non-validating response. Instead, if they reply, "I hear that, I know how important this presentation is for you. Let me know if I can do anything to support you in your preparation," that's a validating response, because it acknowledges your feeling of fear and holds space for it – rather than calling into question your current emotional state.

Can you think of a specific interaction during which you experienced a validating response? Can you think of a specific interaction during which you experienced an invalidating response? How did it feel? I vividly recall my first day back to work after having my second daughter. At the time I was working in an Emergency Department, and my shift was less than ideal for a postpartum mom, 5 p.m. – 2 a.m. I remember confiding in a trusted colleague, Julie, venting my fear that my daughter would not take a bottle or sleep for my partner. I also remember dreading going to pump every two hours, which I also shared with this colleague. As the words tumbled out of my mouth, I remember worrying that she might think less of me for being vulnerable in the workplace, but I will forever remember how validating her response was. Thanks to her reflective listening, the thought of a night divided between pumping and working became more bearable; instead of berating myself for not being able to comfortably wear two totally different hats at once, I could hold onto the sound of her voice saying, "This is hard. I'm here for you." Whatever your fears and frustrations might be, you deserve to receive that same validation from supportive cheerleaders in your life. *You* are worthy of validation.

9   Witkowski, G. (2017). *The effect of emotionally validating and invalidating responses on emotional self-efficacy* (Publication No. 3646) [Doctoral dissertation, Walden University]. *Walden Dissertations and Doctoral Studies Collection.*

10   Someh-Saraie, F. M., & Majreh, S. A. (2019). Comparison of perceived social support, marital satisfaction and empathy in women with postpartum depression and normal. *Journal of Sabzevar University of Medical Sciences, 26*(4), 421–430. https://jsums.medsab.ac.ir/article_1210.html?lang=en

This particular study utilized the Scale of Perceived Social Support, ENRICH Marital Satisfaction Questionnaire, Jolliffe & Farrington Scale of Marital Empathy and Beck Depression Inventory.

Throughout this book I will emphasize self-compassion, a practice all mothers deserve. We tend to be our own worst critics and develop harsh, critical internal voices, like my own worried soundtrack that wondered if my colleague would think less of me when I voiced my fears. To develop emotional wellness, it's important to practice empathizing with the thoughts and feelings you experience as you transition back to work.

Empathic Response: Feeling ecstatic is a healthy and normal response to conversing with Julie (co-worker). I really missed her. Feeling ecstatic to be back at work does not mean that I am not missing my baby or am a *bad mom*. Working makes me a better mom. Now you try (see Appendix C).

AFFIRMING YOUR BADASSERY: "I'VE GOT THIS."

Positive affirmations are another tool to bolster your emotional wellness during your transition back to work. It might take time to move past the awkwardness of positively affirming yourself, but remember, this technique is backed by research. When you tell yourself, "I'm Wonder Woman," it might make you want to laugh, but remember you are *literally* creating new neurological wirings that will produce "happy hormones," such as dopamine and serotonin, that will benefit you during your transition back to work. An affirmation tool, the self-empowerment-affirmation-relaxation (self-EAR), significantly reduces postpartum blues scores.[11] Other studies show that self-affirmation improves problem solving under stress and is associated with psychological well-being.

Ideas for incorporating positive affirmations into your workday:

1. Keep a running list on your phone or work computer to review as needed.

2. Put affirming statements on sticky notes and post them to your bathroom mirror.

3. Say three positive affirmations after the handoff with your childcare provider.

4. Listen to a positively affirming podcast or meditation during your work commute or, for moms who work from home, as part of your transition between roles.

5. Randomly select a positive affirmation from a book of affirmations (there are several on the market specifically for moms!).

Positive affirmations might sound like:

• "I am courageous as a mother and showing up for my child(ren) in the best way I know how."

• "Working and mothering is hard work, but I can do hard things."

---

11   Thitipitchayanant, K., Somrongthong, R., Kumar, R., & Kanchanakharn, N. (2018). Effectiveness of self-empowerment-affirmation-relaxation (Self-EAR) program for postpartum blues mothers: A randomized controlled trial. *Pakistan Journal of Medical Science, 34*(6), 1488–1493. https://doi.org/10.12669/pjms.346.15986

- "A bad moment doesn't make me a bad mom. I'm a good mom who has bad moments. I will model self-forgiveness and grace."

- "I am enough. Today and every day."

- "I trust my motherhood instincts."

MOMS COME BACK: MANAGING SEPARATION ANXIETY

Note: In this section I highlight anxiety experienced by the mother (you) when separating from her child when returning to work. If you are not experiencing any separation anxiety or anticipatory separation anxiety, great! Feel free to move ahead to the next section. If you are experiencing or anticipating separation anxiety upon your return to work, this section is for you.

When I sat down to write this section, my goal was to provide a wealth of research and evidence-based information surrounding the topic of maternal separation.[12] What I found instead was a paucity of outdated academic articles full of inconclusive findings. I went as far as contracting a research assistant with access to a separate database, only to find that her search resulted in a similar outcome.

Here's what I was able to pull together from the few available sources:

- "Mothers must come to terms with their feelings about their maternal role and be prepared to deal with daily separations from their children to continue to pursue employment. This dilemma may produce anxiety and guilt insofar as women must choose between traditionally child-oriented roles and employment opportunities."[13]

- "The literature indicates that parents experience less stress about the care their children receive when their children are nearby and easily accessible to them, as in the ease of on-site daycare."[14]

Quite simply, this is not acceptable. Organizations, academic institutions, and clinicians need a call to action in order to provide a comprehensive understanding on the topic of maternal separation anxiety. Mothers represent a significant portion of the working force and deserve helpful information as well as tools and resources to bolster their transition back to work post-pregnancy.

While we don't have much to work with in terms of peer-reviewed studies, we do have tools available to us. For a start, you can acknowledge and name your thoughts and feelings

---

12   McBride, S., & Belsky, J. (1988). Characteristics, determinants, and consequences of maternal separation anxiety. *Developmental Psychology, 34*(3), 407-414.

13   LeMesurier, L. A. (1995). *The relationship between type of day care arrangement and maternal stress, maternal guilt, and maternal separation anxiety* [Master's thesis, Concordia University]. National Library of Canada.

14   Rabbe, P.H. & Gesser, J.C. (1988). Employer family-supportive policies: Diverse variations on the theme. *Family Relations, 37,* 196-202.

surrounding separating from your child as your return to work nears. What thoughts and feelings do you experience when the topic of separating from your child for work comes up (see Appendix D)? Now, validate and provide a compassionate response to each thought and feeling. Be gentle with yourself!

Here are some tips for ameliorating separation anxiety:

1. Before returning to work, do a trial run with your childcare provider. After each of my pregnancies, I made it a point to do a childcare (daycare) trial run a week ahead of time and only for a half day. This allowed my daughters to get to know her teachers and the teachers to get to know my daughters. I, too, practiced managing my separation anxiety and spent a few hours focusing on self-health. Win-win.

2. Keep a picture of your child on your desk or as your phone screensaver.

3. Allow yourself to feel. Have a good cry if you need it.

4. Have the non-preferred parent do drop-off.

5. Sleep with the blanket that goes to daycare. This can serve as a transitional object and your child might find comfort in your scent during naptime.

6. Lean on your supports. It is *okay* to call a friend or loved one to ventilate about the difficulty separating from your child.

7. Check in with your childcare provider during the day if you need reassurance.

8. Connect with other parents in your child's class, if applicable.

9. Even though I logically knew the limitations of my daughters' receptive language at three months old, I always made it a point to verbalize to them that I would come back.

When you're separated, together…

Now with so many mothers working from home, sometimes physical separation is in short supply – but that only adds a new layer of complication. I often hear about the challenges working moms feel when they are tethered to a single room (or closet!) while their child and caregiver are in another part of the house. They worry about needing to grab something in the fridge, step outside for fresh air or use the bathroom – and what kind of disruption their appearance might cause. Or they describe the superhuman effort necessary to keep focused on their task at hand, while they hear their little one cry, yell or resist sleep on the other side of the door.

Let me just validate how real a struggle this is. No matter how confident you feel in your caregiver's ability, no matter how lucky you feel that you're able to work from home in a (semi-)private space, those diffuse boundaries make it hard to be in the right gear at the right time.

Here are some tips to work through this challenge:

1.   Make your workroom work for you. Do you need emergency snacks in the closet? A full water bottle to start the day?

2.   Coordinate your schedule with your provider: Are there set times they can leave the house? Can your provider communicate with you when they've gone out, or your child is down for a nap and the coast is clear?

3.   As prepared as you may be, you absolutely need to feel free to leave your room. Develop a protocol with the childcare provider. I like to break it down into "pre-during-post."

  a.   Pre: How will you notify the provider that you need to enter the room?

  b.   During: How will you interact with the baby during that time? Will you be a soother or just coming in and out of the room? (If you plan to be the soother, what does that look like?)

  c.   Post: How do you, the baby and the provider transition back into your routine.

4.   Practice, practice, practice. Any change in your routine will be disruptive at first. That's normal and expected. As you expose your baby to these new conditions, you'll both settle into the situation. It may get worse before it gets better, but it *will* get better if you stay consistent.

SO. MANY. HATS. UNDERSTANDING YOUR MANY ROLES

Have you ever tried to rub your belly while patting your head? The game often ends in peals of laughter because it's genuinely difficult for our brain to send two messages to our limbs to do two kinds-of-similar-but-different things at once. The hand that tries to pat might start moving in circles rather than go up and down. The circling hand might lose course and end up patting. Now try to do that with all eight of your arms.

Sometimes that's what being a mother, wife, daughter, sister, friend, colleague, boss, aunt, neighbor…*did I mention…person?*…can feel like. So many working mothers experience *role overload*, when insufficient resources prevent us from taking on all the various roles, the ones expected of us, and the ones to which we *want* to give 100%.

During COVID, role overload was the living, breathing reality for working mothers: the idea of *only* having eight arms seems downright quaint, when thinking back to the early days of lockdown, where moms were asked to be professionals, teachers, caregivers, chefs, epidemiologists, nurses, camp counselors…with no end in sight. While one significant upside of bringing video calls into our homes was the visibility it afforded to the impossible load mothers face, it's cold comfort when compared to the statistics of how working mothers fared in the workplace over this period of time: As each new wave and each new variant added new layers of challenges to the women who were navigating professional and maternal roles, they were more likely to step away from work than working fathers.[15] And among Moms who were able to work, those who did so from home faced increased incidences of depression.[16]

Let me read between the lines of these numbers, and speak to what I suspect was – and continues to be – one of the main sources of tension for working moms since the start of the pandemic: Even as we've been asked to switch between more hats than ever, at greater speeds, it's become more difficult to do so. How do we switch between mom and professional when we've got fifteen minutes between video calls to nurse, clean the spit-up off our top, and hand our crying child off to the babysitter we've hired for the morning because daycare closed after an outbreak? Then, at the end of a day like that, how do we manage to put on our "sibling" hat and check in with our sister, halfway across the country, hoping that her ten free minutes between work and childcare happen to line up with ours?

It can be heartbreaking when we have to prioritize one role for the sake of another – even if we know it's only temporary. I remember how hard it was to not be able to maintain my close ties to my sister during this season because of all the demands pulling at me elsewhere.

---

15   Heggeness, M. L., Fields, J., García Trejo, Y. A., & Schulzetenberg, A. (2021, March 3). Tracking job losses for mothers of school-age children during a health crisis. *United States Census Bureau*. https://www.census.gov/library/stories/2021/03/moms-work-and-the-pandemic.html

16   Burn, E., Tattarini, G., Williams, I., Lombi, L., & Gale, N. K. (2022). Women's experience of depressive symptoms while working from home during the COVID-19 pandemic: Evidence from an international web survey. *Frontiers in Sociology, 7*, 1–11. https://doi.org/10.3389/fsoc.2022.763088

Understanding your own unique role as a working mother can provide insight into how this role aligns or interferes with others. For example, if you have a desire to model working motherhood to your child(ren) by pursuing a career but were raised in a household where there were familial and cultural expectations to play the role of a homemaker, how might this create emotional dissonance and possible psychological distress?

Rather than rushing between these hats on autopilot (which reminds me a little of those plate-spinners in the circus a breath away from letting them all crash down), gain awareness of them by writing all of them down. Next, try identifying internal and external expectations of each. Note: internal expectations are those you have of yourself. External expectations are those you experience from the world around you (e.g., society, family system, work environment, religious community).

For example, under "mother," you might include, "feeding my family healthy meals" – as an internal or external expectation – or both.

Now what about your "professional" hat: If you're supposed to be in the office until 5pm, and then you have a long commute, how does that square with meal prep? If you start your prep at 6pm, how does that fit with your "self" hat (a need to decompress, maybe?) and, once again, your "mother" hat (a need to reconnect with your child).

If you look at your "spouse" hat, maybe an (internal or external) expectation is to spend time after dinner with your partner. How does that fit in with meal clean-up?

This isn't about "solving" a given issue right now; there will be plenty of time for identifying these sticky spots – meal prep is a big one! – and finding ways to adapt. For now, it's just about becoming mindful of just how many hats you're wearing, so you can be kind to yourself when you navigate how to switch between them – on less than ideal amounts of sleep.

Identify your various roles below:

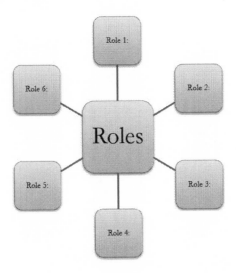

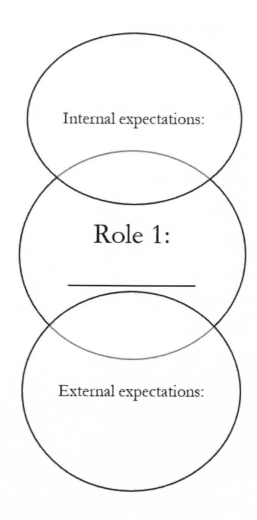

Internal expectations:

Role 1:

_____

External expectations:

REDEFINING YOUR ROLES AND THEIR ACCOMPANYING EXPECTATIONS

Now that you have insight surrounding your roles as well as internal and external expectations of each, how can this information help you? How do you want to redefine your roles as you undergo yet another life transition? How do you want to adjust or maintain internal expectations, and which external expectations do you need to address or insulate yourself from?

Develop confidence in the roles *you* want to nurture. Aunt Sally and your work supervisor do not live your day-to-day life. You deserve to ground yourself in a role that feels authentic and holistic. You are the best mom for your baby. In the occupational section (Chapter 7), I offer additional strategies for how to manage roles in the workplace.

"I think every working mom probably feels the same thing: You go through big chunks of time where you're just thinking. 'This is impossible – oh, this is impossible.' And then you just keep going and keep going. and you sort of do the impossible."

Tina Fey

HELLO GUILT, I SEE YOU! KICK MOM GUILT TO THE CURB

Guilt. Kicking this pesky thing – *guilt* – to the curb is the name of the game. Of the many times I have asked clients over the years, "Does guilt serve you well?" I have yet to hear anyone respond in the affirmative. In fact, it can impact your appetite, mood, and sleep quality. It does *not* serve you. Sure, it is there, but once you notice it, kick it to the curb! Lean into positive thoughts and feelings.

As employed mothers, we often feel alone on an island. Am *I* the *only* one who missed the memo on how to achieve this elusive work-life harmony? Allow me to assure you: you are *not* alone. We have all experienced the feeling of guilt for being at work and guilt for not working while at home. It is a lose-lose mindset. When we heap on ourselves the expectation to *do it all,* and external sources keep on piling shovel after shovel of additional guilt, eventually the weight of reality hits us: we simply cannot meet these expectations. The emotional dissonance that results from that realization often manifests itself in the form of guilt, that crispy fried feeling we all know so well.

What do we instinctively do in response to that crushing guilt? Multitasking! We double-down by relaxing the boundaries between work and home. You might think, "Well, maybe if I try to answer this email during playtime…" When you write an underdeveloped response to a work email while being partially present with your infant, you can feel like you are failing in both arenas, especially when this is not how you envisioned yourself as an "ideal employee" or "mindful mother."

Now we bring a new layer of complexity into the picture: you may even have feelings about your feelings! Have you ever felt guilty for being exhausted or agitated? That's an example of having feelings about your feelings. Let me set the record straight. You have a right to feel exhausted, and it is *normal* to want a break! First and foremost, be gentle and kind to yourself. Employed motherhood is *hard* and *exhausting.* You are not alone in this. Combating guilt takes intentional action and practice; below, I provide tangible ways to mitigate employed mom guilt. Try some of these strategies and find what works for you. Remember, guilt does not serve you. Lean into the positive.

Tangible Ways to Mitigate *Employed Mom Guilt*

Self Compassion.

Guilt can eat you alive. Forgive youself before guilt develops into somethingmore destructive than it already is. You deserve kindness and compassion instead of harsh internal self-talk for your choices or circumstances. When "I'm a bad mom, employee, friend, etc." intrudes, try to gently remind yourself all of the ways you are showing up in each of those roles and the reasons for your current functioning in those roles.

Cling to Your Values.

Create a list of your values and prioritize your behavior/decision making accordingly. For example, if you value spending quality time outdoors with your family, block out a time on the weekend to ensure that this happens. If volunteering or household maintenance are a lower on the priority list, then those activities should occur after quality time outdoors. Finally, commit to living your value system! This will require revisiting your list of values *often* (perhaps post a copy on your fridge) as well as setting boundaries.

Positively Affirm.

Develop a set of positive affirmations and memorize them (or keep a list in your phone) for times when negative self-talk takes over. Some positive affirmations might sounds like, "I am a perfectly good enough mom." "My best is enough." "I have done hard things before. I can do them again."

Tangible Ways to Mitigate *Employed Mom Guilt (cont.)*

Hide. Unfollow. Repeat.

If social media highlight reels (which are *not* reality by the way) bring you to tears or you find that particualrly person or group consistently triggers you, give yourself permission to hide, unfollow, or block. *You* get to choose what you consume. Consume what builds you up and helps you feel connected to that person, group, or community.

Your Outlook Matters.

Keep persepctive that you will never abdicate your place as your child's mother. No one can replace you. Children will not grow up and fault you for not having the "perfect" this-or-that. What children most remember is how they feel, and if there was *connection*. Lean into the positive and breathe out the guilt.

Ask for (and *accept)* Help.

I learned this lesson after my second pregnancy, and oh how I wish I had asked for - and accepted - help sooner. It takes a village to raise a child, and trying to "do it all" will only lead to exhaustion and burn out. Trust me, I have been there. You will likely start a trend in asking family, friends, and neighbors which will benefit both parties as others, too, will ask for help. Win-win.

A Negative Feedback Loop

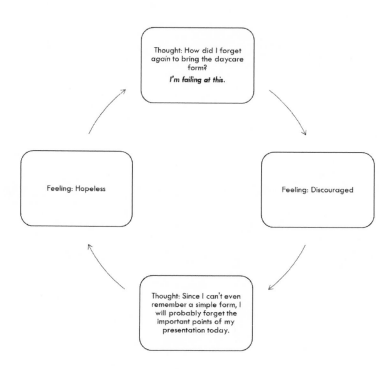

Where in this feedback loop can you positively intervene?

Positively disrupting the negative feedback loop.

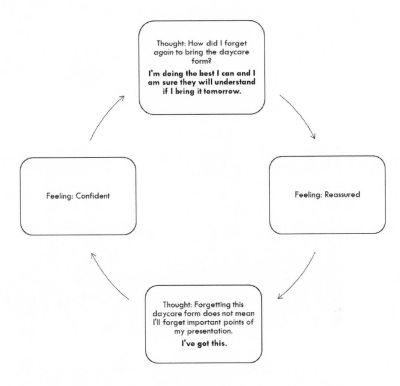

A Negative Feedback Loop

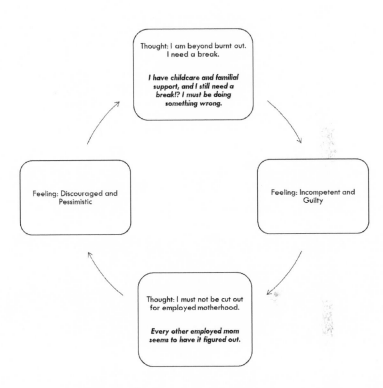

Where in this feedback loop can you positively intervene?

Positively disrupting the negative feedback loop.

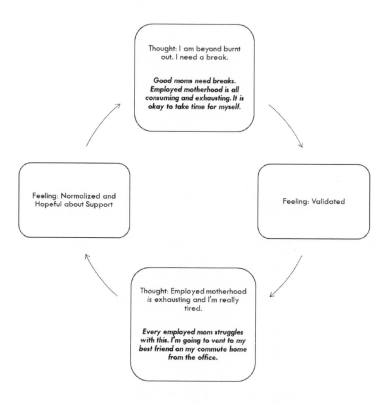

Kick Mom
Guilt to the
CURB!

STRESS: EFFECTIVE WAYS TO MANAGE HIGH STRESS DURING THIS LIFE TRANSITION

Tingling in every limb, blood boiling slowly through each vein. And then, something happens: a bubbling from the deep pit of my stomach rises up into my throat like an Icelandic geyser. A scream so primal and animalistic words cannot describe. My shoulders tingle and I ball up my fists to resist pulling my hair. The primal scream.

Transitioning to employed motherhood is *stressful*. Juggling *two* jobs – your office job and then coming home to care for a little one – can be soul crushingly exhausting. You can either allow the stress to paralyze you, resulting in physical and psychological distress, or you can learn how to manage stress in healthy ways.

After two transitions back to work post-pregnancy, I quickly learned that if I wanted any semblance of self-health in the world of working motherhood, I had to make changes, and *fast*. There will be times when there will be too many tasks and *not* enough time. One evening after work I recall searching around for my car keys, only to realize I had left them in the ignition. Then, I went to look for the milk, which was *not* in the fridge but in the pantry! That same evening, I remember having a complete meltdown because I had forgotten an important deadline, had not eaten since 11 a.m., and neglected to schedule an important medical appointment for myself. After what felt like a Groundhog's Day loop, I finally took some time to develop a healthy list of ways to manage stress.

That list proved to be one of my most powerful secret weapons in establishing my equilibrium as a professional and as a mom. However, in order to deploy it successfully, I needed to become acutely familiar with how the early signs of stress show up in me. Otherwise, how could I know when and to what extent to increase self-health practices?

What are *your* stress indicators?

Let's go a step further. What are your *early, moderate,* and *late* signs of stress? For me, I struggled, at least in the beginning of my transition, to recognize signs of increasing stress levels until I was crispy fried and ready to serve on a steaming hot plate. Thankfully, for me and all of those around me, this learning curve was short: when I started getting extra snappy at the slightest (perceived) provocation, when I couldn't find my sunglasses that were perched on top of my head, those were signs that my stress level was on the rise. When it escalated to a moderate level, my shoulders and neck would tense up, turning me into a lumbering football player; I'd find myself raising my voice when my expectations weren't immediately met (partner and kids, *watch out!*), and spend my nights tossing and turning. The flashing warning signs of the trouble zone came in the form of a relentless eye tic or migraine.

The way we manifest stress is highly personal, so I encourage my clients to use a scaling exercise (outlined on the next page) to identify their stress levels. One way to approach the development of this scale is to identify physical, mental, and emotional signs of stress.

Physical signs might include:

- fatigue
- insomnia/hyposomnia
- physical tension
- teeth clenching
- headaches
- gastrointestinal issues

Mental signs might include:

- brain fog
- forgetfulness
- poor memory
- poor concentration
- distorted thinking (catastrophizing, binary thinking, discounting the positives)

Emotional signs might include:

- mood fluctuation
- tearfulness
- agitation

If you believe your stress extends beyond the situational or is persistent, consult with your physician or mental health professional.

Get to Know Your Stress Levels

What automatic thoughts do you experience and how do you feel at each level of stress?

1 = minimal stress / 10 = severe

1

2

3

4

5

6

7

8

9

10

DANIELLE VAN WAGENEN, MSW

Back to Work Following a Traumatic Birth, While ALSO Caring for a High Need Baby

Danielle Van Wagenen was 34 weeks pregnant, finishing her Master of Social Work Degree at the University of Washington. She chalked up swelling, fatigue, and anxiety to nearing the end of a not-so-easy pregnancy. Her last two blood pressure readings at her OB/GYN appointments were elevated but her doctor assured her that she would be closely monitored. She also completed a urine sample, which she would later learn was saturated with protein. Her OB/GYN was out of the office until Monday and over the weekend Danielle continued to feel increasingly panicky and unwell. To err on the side of caution, she went to a nearby urgent care where a comprehensive examination was completed. Her blood pressure was elevated and there were traces of protein in her urine. She was directed to the hospital where she was diagnosed with preeclampsia with severe features, admitted to labor/delivery, and induced. After minimal progression, Danielle delivered her son via cesarean section. Hemolysis, elevated liver enzymes, and low platelet count (HELLP syndrome) was diagnosed shortly after delivery as well as Intrauterine Growth Restriction (IUGR). "I blamed myself for my son's prematurity. I felt that my body did not work."

The days, weeks, and months following her son's birth were a blur. Danielle vaguely remembers the ambulance ride when he was transferred from her hospital to one with a NICU and the searing anxiety of knowing he was in another ambulance without her. They spent several months in the NICU where Danielle was on bedrest given her fall risk. "This was not the plan. I needed to finish my program and begin my clinical residency in three months."

Birth trauma transformed into severe postpartum anxiety and obsessive-compulsive disorder. After they were discharged, Danielle purchased a scale to weigh her son and spent hours researching lactation to ensure she was providing the most nutrient- and calorie-dense milk.

Danielle's son's medical care became a full-time job consisting of one to two medical appointments per day: physical therapy, occupational therapy, nutrition consultations, endocrinology, gastroenterology, and NICU follow-ups. No one provided her with resources to help her file for social security disability, which she assumed was because her providers took for granted she already knew how, given her training as a social worker. She wished that someone had provided some tangible, supportive resources.

The Transition to Childcare

By nine months postpartum, Danielle was able to consider a return to the workforce as the frequency of medical appointments lessened – six months later than she had planned. When offered a position as a part-time hospital social worker, as active military she began the enrollment process of the on-base childcare. Anxiety surrounding her son's nutrition and calorie intake continued to manifest as high anxiety, worry thoughts. "It was really hard. I was worried that they would not feed him all of his food and therefore not make his calorie count. I was afraid he would become 'failure to thrive,' and it would be my fault." Although logically Danielle realized that this was an irrational thought, the self-blame became automatic until she was able to process with a perinatal therapist. She was able to alleviate some of the angst surrounding her son's diet by coordinating with the Child Development Center to approve high-caloric food, an exception from the center's typical food menu. However, after his few first days at daycare her son became ill, which developed into pneumonia. After months of repeated illnesses, Danielle and her partner hired a part-time nanny. Although financially burdensome, Danielle felt this was the safest option to support her son's physical health. Danielle encourages employed moms not to feel bad for doing what you need to do. "Always put your family first. You cannot be everything for everyone. That is okay."

What Helped Danielle Heal

Danielle focused on comprehensive healing, which included emotional, physical, social, and spiritual wellness. To bolster her emotional health, Danielle found a perinatal mental health therapist (PMH-C) who was trained in eye movement desensitization reprocessing therapy (EMDR) and a reproductive psychiatrist who prescribed her medication for postpartum anxiety and post-traumatic stress disorder. She integrated essential oils and breathwork into her routine for stress management. In order to guide decisions in everyday life and insulate from negative external pressures, she thoughtfully wrote out her values system. Danielle focused on coordinating care with physicians who were strength-based, and physically, she focused on increasing the quantity and quality of her sleep, improving hydration, incorporating exercise, practicing clean eating, and undergoing physical therapy for nerve damage.

To take the edge off, she outsourced whenever possible, even when asking for help was foreign to someone who had previously *done it all*. Socially, she found solace in the support of her partner. He consistently partnered with parenting duties, washed her breast pump, took the lead on coordinating medical appointments, and made Danielle's work lunches. This meant the world to Danielle. She leaned on girlfriends, her mom, and sisters who provided unconditional love and support. Spiritually, Danielle found peace in a bigger plan for her difficult transition to motherhood. She purchased the *Calm* phone app and completed daily meditations. Danielle found ways to educate her nanny on her son's needs which allowed her to relax. She knew her anxiety was becoming a bit more manageable when she discontinued constantly checking her video camera and checking in with her nanny.

"I experienced birth trauma.
I needed to heal before
going back to work.
I was trying to
transition amidst
unresolved trauma."

-DANIELLE VAN WAGENEN-

MINDFULNESS

Mindfulness is not just a trendy word. Defined by the American Psychological Association as "awareness of one's internal states and surroundings," mindfulness can concretely reduce stress; multiple studies highlight the measurable benefits of mindfulness exercises such as meditation, breathwork, and visualization in reducing stress.[17] To practice mindfulness, you don't need to sign up for a weeklong mountain retreat (although that sounds tempting); you don't even need to stress yourself out in search of hours of free time. All mindfulness takes is a few minutes every day. Sitting at your desk chair for two minutes while monitoring your breathing, for example, can provide mindful grounding to the here-and-now and calm the nervous system, which repays you by allowing you more quality time for the rest of the day.

Employed motherhood requires us to lean in, more than ever, to tools and strategies that effectively decrease stress. As my stress during working motherhood reached unmanageable levels, I turned to this practice to prevent countless anxiety attacks. I remember sitting in my car at my daughter's daycare parking lot after a grueling day at work. The last thing I wanted was to reunite with her while caught up in all of my frenetic energy. In less than five minutes, I completed a body scan meditation: as my stress dropped from a level 9 to a level 5, I could greet my sweet daughter with warm hugs and kisses. As the oxytocin washed over me, it magnified the impact of the de-stressing exercise. Body scan meditation for the win!

For those of you who work from home, the diffuse boundaries between "work" and "life" make this kind of mindfulness activity all the more valuable – and for those of you who work from home while a caregiver watches your child in another room of the house, doubly so. A short ritual that marks your transition between one hat and the other can help orient your body and mind to its new reality.

Natalie Bracco outlines several tips for meditating for busy working moms that include (1) finding a suitable time, (2) selecting a quiet spot in your home or office, (3) making sure you are in a comfortable position, (4) meditating on an empty stomach to prevent drowsiness, (5) focusing on proper breathing, and, afterwards, (6) opening your eyes gently and slowly.

Drawing Upon Mindfulness During [Potentially] High Stress Situations

There will be acute peaks of stress during your transition to employed motherhood. In fact, you will become an expert in managing stressful situations – one of the many skills perfected in motherhood you can transfer to the workplace. (Think about how a daily breathing routine will come in handy when you're up against a deadline or confronting a cranky colleague.) From sleepless nights to disrupted routines, there are ample strategies to mindfully manage influxes of stress.

---

17   Corliss, J. (2014, January 82). Mindfulness meditation may ease anxiety, mental stress. *Harvard Health Publishing*. health.harvard.edu/blog/mindfulness-meditation-may-ease-anxiety-mental-stress-201401086967

The day following a sleepless night. Teething, sickness, meeting a work deadline, or insomnia are some common situations that lead to a sleepless night. These nights will happen; they are inevitable. My hope is that they will be few and far between, but when they occur, you will be prepared. Put simply, tired you will remain, but you can go about your day managing your stress in healthy ways, rather than coping through destructive mechanisms.

Here is what I recommend:

1. **Keep perspective.** This was a bad night, not a bad baby or parent. Have you ever had a bad night's sleep? So do babies.

2. **Communicate with your partner.** Consider a "divide and conquer" approach so you can achieve at least half a night's sleep. Some rest is better than none. Remember, agitation can come with exhaustion so be kind to one another. You are doing your best and your best is enough.

3. **Validate.** Remember what we reviewed above? This is the time to validate your emotions. These sleepless nights *are* hard, and your thoughts and feelings are valid.

4. **Positively affirm.** Affirm your commitment and perseverance.

5. **Lean into the positive.** When exhaustion takes over it can cause binary thinking, catastrophizing, and negativity. Positively reframe your stress.

6. **Intentionally protect and preserve the following night's sleep.** Go to bed early. Call upon the help of family or friends to nap or sleep in.

7. **Maintain self-awareness in the workplace.**

8. **Fill your cup in other ways.** Stay hydrated, eat a healthy meal,[18] or listen to uplifting music.

The beginning and the end (*morning and evening routines*). Sleep – getting there and staying there – might be a source of stress in your home. Even as you settle into a rhythm with morning and night routines (i.e., bedtime), there will be times when – for whatever reason – the routine is thrown off. Perhaps you have to arrive early to daycare or stay late at work, immunizations delay naptime, a family event causes you to return home later than expected, or a reason you simply cannot figure out (i.e., baby is fighting sleep).

---

18   Gonzalez, M. J., & Miranda-Massari, J. R. (2014). Diet and stress. *The Psychiatric Clinics of North America, 37*(4), 579–589. https://doi.org/10.1016/j.psc.2014.08.004

Here is what I recommend:

1. **Adjust the baseline.** Mornings and evenings are often times when you are the most stressed and tired. Be patient and kind to yourself, your partner, and your little one. You all are doing the best you can.

2. **Routines are guidelines, not meant to feel rigid.** If possible, allow for some flexibility. One example might be to shorten the bedtime routine if you are starting later than usual. Consider shortening bath time or reducing the number of books you read. Children thrive with routines and structure, but some flexibility is also beneficial.

3. **Discuss contingency plans with your partner *in advance.*** Trying to develop a contingency plan when in crisis mode will only make matters worse. Plan and discuss – in advance – a few contingency plans to try when routines go awry.

4. **Know when you need to take a break or call on your partner to step in.** Remember the stress level chart you filled out? Determine at which level you need to take a break or call for help. Do not let yourself be at the point of panic or ugly crying before implementing a stress reliever.

5. **Plan ahead as much as possible.** For example, pack your meals, pump, and daycare bag the night before. A little planning can save copious amounts of time as you try to get out the door. I used to joke with myself and my partner, "I am *not* an octopus! I only have two hands!" It is true. You, too, are not an octopus.

6. **Acceptance.** Sometimes routines do not go as planned. Take a deep breath and move forward.

Unexpected Visitors. If visitors arrive at an inconvenient or stressful time such as naptime, this can induce stress.

1. If you (and they) feel comfortable, utilize their help! If Aunt Susan shows up unannounced, perhaps she can provide some relief and help clean while you manage naptime.

2. Prevent unexpected visitors by placing a sign on your front door before stressful periods. In our neighborhood, I remember delivery workers ringing the doorbell at 9 p.m. I was repeatedly frustrated and anxious about the possibility of this waking up our four-month-old. As soon as I placed the "sleeping baby" sign on the door, I never heard the doorbell ring again.

3. If it is too much for you, give yourself permission to answer the door and quickly explain that this is not a good time.

4. Have your partner handle the door. Quickly triage the response and then let your partner take the wheel.

5. If anxious about how your house presents, remember that *no* house with a little one is tidy. (Marie Kondo's included!) If anyone tells you otherwise, they are lying. If you want to have a part of your house tidy for visitors, consider keeping the front door and sitting area tidy. You can limit the visit to this portion of your house.

Breathwork, another mindful technique to use during high periods of stress, is a reliable way to calm your nervous system. Breathwork is available to you whenever you need: breathe in the stress and release on the exhale. Focus on breathing through your nose and out through your mouth. One strategy is to imagine your favorite hot entrée freshly cooked. Slowly relish the smell (in through your nose) of the food with your inhale and cool it down with your exhale (out through your mouth).

Another breathing technique that can regulate your nervous system is known as *Square Breathing* because each of the four "sides" (parts) lasts for four seconds each:

1. Inhale for four seconds

2. Hold for four seconds

3. Exhale for four seconds

4. Hold for four seconds

A Mindful Meditative Exercise to Try

Find a quiet place outside. It can be as simple as sitting on the patio or sitting on your front steps. Take several deep breaths and ground your feet to the ground. Correct your posture and relax your shoulders. What are four things you see? What are three sounds you hear? What are two things you feel (the wind on your face, the texture of your shirt, the texture of your chair)? What is one thing you smell? Hopefully you are now mindfully grounded in the here-and-now, one with your environment.

Mood Tracking Apps!

- Daylio
- Moodkit
- Mood Track Diary
- Moodfit
- Worry Watch (anxiety)

Coloring

Coloring is an additional way to reduce stress that requires little time commitment. There is something cathartic about allowing yourself to scribble on good old-fashioned paper with coloring pencils. This is also a practice you can do *with* your little one(s) as they grow.

Exercise and Body Movement

Exercise has been shown not only to reduce stress but improve mood.[19] I know, time is a real barrier, but I encourage you to reframe *how* and *when* you move your body. Take the stairs instead of the elevator, take five minutes to stretch, integrate a few yoga poses into your morning routine, or walk during your lunch break. Five minutes of body movement is progress! Endorphins will serve you well. In Chapter 4, I will cover the benefits of exercise as well as easy ways to incorporate body movement into your daily routine.

Music

Music is an effective and versatile tool for stress management. Whether you need a song to calm your nervous system when you are pumping during your lunch break, to motivate you to exercise, or simply to boost your mood, music is an excellent resource. Compile various playlists – in advance – in preparation. They can be lifesaving and your future self will thank you for it! The top of my playlist when I need a reminder of why I am a working mother? "Run the World (Girls)" by Beyoncé and "Superwoman" by Alicia Keys.

Preventative Self-Health

Preventative measures such as fueling your body with nutrient-dense food, prioritizing sleep, and managing hydration are additional protective factors to guard against unmanageable stress and/or a mood disorder. Name some healthy outlets for stress management that resonate with you and write them below.

1. _____

2. _____

3. _____

---

19   Jackson, E. M. (2013). FACSM stress relief: The role of exercise in stress management. CSM's. *Health & Fitness Journal, 17*(3), 14–19. https://doi.org/10.1249/FIT.0b013e31828cb1c9

PMADS: PERINATAL MOOD AND ANXIETY DISORDERS

Monitor your mental health and seek out professional help if you suspect you are experiencing a postpartum mood or anxiety disorder, also known as PMADs. One in seven women experience a postpartum mood or anxiety disorder – and that number spiked during COVID. Let me say it again for those in the back. *One in seven women!* You *do not* have to suffer in silence! I was beyond grateful for therapy and psychiatry when experiencing postpartum anxiety after the birth of my second daughter. On the following page, I include some helpful information from Postpartum Support International.

> *"The mission of Postpartum Support International is to promote awareness, prevention and treatment of mental health issues related to childbearing in every country worldwide."*[20]

Some common symptoms of *postpartum anxiety* include: constant worry, feeling that something bad is going to happen, racing thoughts, disturbances of sleep and appetite, inability to sit still, and physical symptoms like dizziness, hot flashes, and nausea. Some common symptoms of *postpartum depression* include: feelings of anger or irritability, lack of interest in the baby, appetite and sleep disturbance, crying and sadness, feelings of guilt, shame or hopelessness, loss of interest, joy or pleasure in things you used to enjoy, and possible thoughts of harming yourself or the baby. There is additional information on Postpartum.net on other postpartum mood and anxiety disorders such as postpartum obsessiveness, postpartum posttraumatic stress disorder, bipolar mood disorders, and postpartum psychosis. If you are concerned that you meet criteria for one of these disorders, Postpartum.net has a list of Certified Perinatal Mental Health (PMH-C) professionals in your region. You can also consult with your regional PSI Coordinator for reproductive psychiatrists in your region or state.

Research has shown that the more hours a mom works, the more at risk she is to develop depressive symptoms and parental stress, along with a small decline in overall health.[21] I share this with you not to play fortuneteller and foresee a future diagnosis of depression upon your return to a full-time work schedule but to highlight that you are at *risk* for one. If you are working long days, taking care of yourself needs to be a top priority. Intentionally implementing strategies, coping mechanisms, and supports into your everyday life can prevent the development of a mood

Postpartum Support International:

- Connection to Resources
- Online Support Groups
- Peer Mentor Program

Call or text
1-800-944-4773

---

20   Postpartum Support International. (n.d.). *Pregnancy & postpartum mental health overview*. Retrieved December 26, 2020, from https://www.postpartum.net/learn-more/pregnancy-postpartum-mental-health/

21   Harrison, L. J., & Ungerer, J. A. (2002). Maternal employment and infant-mother attachment security at 12 months postpartum. *Developmental Psychology, 38*(5), 758–773. https://doi.org/10.1037//0012-1649.38.5.758

Chatterji, P., Markowitz, S., & Brooks-Gunn, J. (2013). Effects of early maternal employment on maternal health and well-being. *Journal of Population Economics, 26*(1), 285–301. https://doi.org/10.1007/s00148-012-0437-5.

disorder or unmanageable parental stress. If you do not feel yourself after using some of the strategies outlined in this book, consult with a professional.

There is help. You can feel better. You deserve to feel better. After a few postpartum sessions with clients, I often hear them saying things like, "Why did I wait so long to get help?!", "I did not *consider* the possibility that I could actually *enjoy* my career *and* motherhood!", "No one told me it would be this hard. I wish I had gotten help sooner."

As women and mothers, we not only say *should* to ourselves but also incorporate a *ton* of negative *if/ thens* into our thinking, especially when it comes to asking for help. *If* I ask for help, *then* it means I am weak. *If* I ask for help, *then* I am not enough. The reality is you are strong. You are enough. Stop the *shoulds,* the *justs* and the *if/ thens* and get out of your own way.

COURTNEY MCPHIE

A Thoughtful Approach to Managing Postpartum Mental Health

As a mother of three children, Courtney is no stranger to motherhood! Courtney teaches High School English in a highly revered school district in the Washington, DC Metro Area. She recently transitioned to employed motherhood after giving birth to her third child, Florence. Prior to motherhood, Courtney was diagnosed with depression and obsessive-compulsive disorder. She also experienced postpartum depression following the births of her first two children. Given her history of mental illness, Courtney proactively prepared for her third postpartum experience and developed a thoughtful plan to manage her postpartum mental health. This plan consisted of (1) initiating services with a therapist and psychiatrist, (2) coordinating a postpartum psychiatric plan with her OB/GYN, (3) building and utilizing a coping skills toolbox, and (4) identifying and managing stressors.

Initiating Services with a Therapist and Psychiatrist

Courtney developed rapport with a local therapist and primarily focused on recognizing warning signs for postpartum depression and obsessive-compulsive triggers and healthily managing stressors. In our conversation, she emphasized the importance of learning the difference between the baby blues (short term) and postpartum depression. She also recommended educating your birth partner on the warning signs as they can intervene if necessary. Courtney consulted with her psychiatrist even before pregnancy to confirm that her psychiatric medication was safe to continue while pregnant. Ongoing check-ins with her psychiatrist provided another layer of support and assessment of her symptoms.

Coordinating a Postpartum Psychiatric Plan with Her OB/GYN

Courtney started the conversation about her history of mental health at the onset with her OB/GYN. Because she had conversations about elevated risk for postpartum depression, her OB/GYN was prepared to provide treatment when she needed an appointment to discuss her psychiatric medications sooner than their three-week postpartum visit. Her OB/GYN was well versed with her psychiatric history thanks to Courtney's vigilance in discussing it with her throughout her pregnancy.

Building and Utilizing a Coping Skills Toolbox

Courtney built and utilized a comprehensive coping skills toolbox that included hydration, sleep (a minimum five-hour stretch each night), walks, podcasts, and a predictable routine.

Identification and Management of Stressors

Through therapy, Courtney identified several stressors in the postpartum period: childcare, social isolation, marital strain, and stress. Having been raised by a stay-at-home-mom and without models of other employed mothers who had healthily utilized childcare, Courtney experienced negative, intrusive thoughts about leaving her baby in the hands of a childcare provider, such as, "What kind of a mother leaves her baby?" Courtney tested these negative thoughts by asking close friends and family members who had attended daycare. Her husband, for example, had attended daycare as an infant and toddler. He reminded Courtney that one of his best friends is a boy he attended daycare with, that he is a well-adjusted adult, and that his relationship with his mother is secure and close. During her daughter's transition to daycare, she experienced an increase in anxious, obsessive thoughts that sounded like, "Will they follow my daughter's naptime schedule?" and "Will they feed her properly?" All of the *what if's* were getting in the way. She became more equipped in recognizing when negative thoughts were actually just her OCD talking.

Prior to transitioning to childcare, Courtney found sitting down with her partner to examine logistics helpful. Together, they were able to maximize their leave benefits to keep Florence home until she was four months old.

Social isolation was another stress that Courtney quickly addressed as she transitioned to employed motherhood. Although she felt *physically* okay, she was not yet emotionally well, and the social isolation that accompanies the postpartum period certainly didn't help. She *asked* friends to visit; she did not wait for them to ask. She actively reached out to friends, brought her hand pump with her when she went out, and enjoyed socializing with her girlfriends. "It made me feel alive." Courtney emphasizes the importance of building and leaning on supportive people during this major life transition.

Marital strain was a third stressor, as many moms can relate. "Becky," she told me during our interview, "it's easy to feel resentment. It is important to vocalize your needs to your partner and remember this season is temporary." She used the questions, "Why am I in this marriage?" and "Why do I love him?" to remember all of the good things about their relationship. She also found solace in venting to girlfriends who validated and normalized what she was experiencing. Courtney and her partner made it a point to spend time together, even if they were just sitting together watching a television program. They stayed connected throughout the day through online chatting and text messaging.

Caregiving demands. "There were a million balls in the air. I was so exhausted. I was barely making it to bed." In an effort to combat caregiver fatigue, Courtney relied on her sister's wisdom that, "Everything is a circus until the baby turns one." She reminded herself the constant care of a baby would eventually relent. She continued to focus on her mental health in the meantime and survived Florence's first year. She encourages employed mothers to remember that it takes time to get used to your child being with a childcare provider. It is a hard transition, but it gets better.

"You will NOT find a perfect daycare You CAN find a place where they take good Care of your Child"

—Courtney McPhie—

Dimension of Wellness: Spiritual

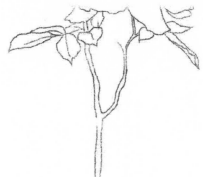

NOTES

CHAPTER 2

SPIRITUAL WELLNESS

When mothers return to work to answer a call for greater purpose, they often describe it as a deeply spiritual experience. One of my girlfriends described her calling to serve her community as a firefighter. This fire within her propelled her back to work with vigor and, in her first two months, her experience saving lives only intensified the flame. Every one's call back to work is intensely personal and may be woven from several different threads. Whether yours is to provide for your family, normalize working motherhood, contribute passionately to your field, or any other reason, take a moment to ask yourself, "What is fueling *your* fire within? What is your why?"

The context of COVID has only raised the stakes on the question of "why." Being surrounded by death and grief – collectively, if not personally – may have influenced you, giving that moment of pause to remember "life is precious."

Take some time to reflect on how the pandemic impacted – and perhaps still impacts – your day-to-day, how it shifted your "why" and how you relate to working motherhood. Did you decide to pull out of the workforce because you took on a caregiving role and that was important to you? Is your "why" now coming back from that? Or was your "why" to stay in the workforce because it had meaning to you to show up as a physician to care for COVID patients and model that for your children? Or did you stay in the workforce because of financial constraints, or a fear of losing precious professional ground? Did you first become a working mother *during* the pandemic, and are now trying to find your footing in two worlds that *both* look very different from the ones we expected?

I know I can't come close to fitting all your diverse "whys" in a book – I can't even envision a fraction of all the unique motivations each of my readers might carry. But I can say that they all deserve to be honored, and that practice starts inside of you.

EMPLOYED MOTHERHOOD AS A SPIRITUAL PRACTICE

Consider your transition to employed motherhood a spiritual process. (If this dimension of wellness resonates with you, read on! If not, skip ahead.) Even as you navigate the many practical concerns of returning to work, give yourself time to imagine the opportunity for spiritual growth that working motherhood provides: gratitude, love, generosity, patience, and mindfulness. I have distinct memories of exhaustion, stress, and fear during early periods of transitioning back to work. I also have distinct memories of spiritual growth: immense gratitude reuniting with my daughter after several complex clinical cases, patience as my daughter awoke multiple times to nurse as she fought through her first cold, love as I relished in her milestones after work and on the weekends, and mindfulness as I practiced staying in the here-and-now when work anxiety pulled me toward the future. How would you describe your spiritual growth thus far as you transition to working motherhood?

Gratitude

Amidst the stress and chaos that ensues when you are in the thick of managing motherhood and a career, you might find an unexpected ally: gratitude. In researching the tangible effects of gratitude, researchers have shown that: "Not only is gratitude a warm and uplifting way to feel, but it also benefits the body as well. People who experience gratitude cope better with stress, recover more quickly from illness, and enjoy more robust physical health, including lower blood pressure and better immune function..." [22]

While at times it might be impossible to come up for air, lean into gratitude. It is okay to embrace gratitude for being back at work, enjoying your coworkers, immersing yourself in your occupational passions, establishing a routine, and talking with other adults. It is also okay to lean into feelings of gratitude when you reunite each day with your little one, savor the little fingers and toes, spend quality time in the evening, relish in the giggles, and make bedtime extra special.

When negative thoughts and feelings take over, take a step back; gratitude begins with mindfulness, so tune in to your surroundings. I created a gratitude journal for new moms, *Thankful for Motherhood: A Gratitude Journal for New Moms*, to serve as an additional support in this area. Whether you utilize my journal or even a note on your phone, try keeping track of your gratitudes. Take a few minutes in the morning, midday, and evening to take note of moments of gratitude. Your future self (and little one) will thank you for it!

Love

There *is* enough space to love both your child *and* career. Oftentimes – as employed women – we are taught that we have to choose one or the other. Lies. You *can* love both and neither has to compete with the other. This is a life stage when your deep love of two worlds intersects. Even if you despise your job, this is an opportunity to manifest your love and commitment to provide for your little one financially. If you do not love your job, is it possible to lean into aspects of it that you appreciate?

Another opportunity to practice love during this transitional period is by loving yourself. Working motherhood is not easy. It is tiresome, stressful, emotionally draining, and the list goes on. There is no better time than now to show yourself some love. Be kind to yourself. Love yourself. What does your self-talk sound like? Is it loving? Is it self-compassionate? If not, start practicing self-love. You matter, mama. You are worthy of love, too.

---

22   Stern, S., & Emmons, R. (2013). *What is gratitude?* Yale School of Medicine. https://medicine.yale.edu/childstudy/services/community-and-schools-programs/center-for-emotional-intelligence/

Patience

By now I am sure you are well versed in the old adage, "Patience is a virtue." Well, this old adage could not ring truer than in employed motherhood. There will be ample opportunities to practice this spiritual tenet: watching the clock as your final meeting begins to threaten daycare pickup, trying out the tenth bottle or pacifier your baby refuses, taking a deep breath as your partner gets on your last nerve, or even hearing news that the pediatrician is running over thirty minutes behind schedule. Practice patience with yourself, mama. You are juggling a million balls in the air. While you offer patience to all of those around you, make sure you are saving some for yourself.

I remember a particularly hellacious day at work. I had not slept well in days and my daughter was teething. Not just her top and bottom teeth, her *canines!* For comfort, she was going on a solid two weeks of cluster feeding. Need I say more? I was *exhausted!* I received notice that I was to evaluate a psychiatric patient who – I knew – would require me to stay well beyond my shift. Not the day. Initially I was angry, then begrudging, then accepting, and eventually softened in that I truly love the work that I do.

I drew upon *why* I worked and the importance of helping those in psychiatric crises. What stood out more, though, was that patience extended not only to this patient, but to my colleagues, my teething baby, my husband, my older daughter, and *myself.* The hours that I spent at the hospital and the hours I spent nursing my teething baby into the wee hours of morning highlighted this spiritual manifestation of my working motherhood. Patience really is a virtue, is it not? During one of the interviews, an employed mother – with conviction – told me, "How foolish I was to believe that my journey was on *my* time. It's not. It's on God's."

Meditative Prayer

When a mother transitions back to work, meditative prayer as a spiritual practice can serve not only as a comfort but also a grounding tool. When your threshold for stress and uncertainty is pushed beyond your wildest imagination, meditative prayer can offer comfort from your higher power and provide grounding when you feel out of control. Trust me, I have been there. I remember all too well those moments when you do not know if you have anything left to give. And, somehow, you lean into your higher power and find the energy, stamina, or insight you didn't know existed. Full disclosure, I am not religious and do not subscribe to any particular spiritual ideology, but I did experience moments when I leaned into some higher power during moments of need. Consider the following if meditative prayer is a spiritual practice you would like to add to your toolbox as you transition to employed motherhood:

- Is there a particular part of your daily routine that this practice can be integrated into?

- Allow yourself to find a comfortable position.

- What would you like to communicate with your higher power?

- What would you like to receive?

- Would it make sense to also utilize meditative prayer as a gratitude practice?

- How can you identify and express the meaning you find in the hard moments of employed motherhood? What can you learn from those hardships?

- In a moment of stress, what would your higher power tell you?

- What would a deceased loved one tell you?

LEAN INTO SPIRITUAL LEADERS

If spirituality is an integral part of your wellness, consider leaning into spiritual leaders who inspire you. Better yet, there are spiritual leaders who have experienced employed motherhood. Breathe in the inspiration you feel from these women and learn from them. It truly takes a village. Learning from employed mothers who have paved the way can provide wisdom for how you also can excel during this difficult season of life. We need one another to succeed.

Dr. Hawa Abdi

Dr. Hawa Abdi (1947-2020)[23] – affectionately known as Mama Hawa – was a deeply spiritual woman, a mother of four children, and OB-GYN. For many years, she mothered and protected Somalis during war, displacement, and famine. She founded the Dr. Hawa Abdi Foundation (DHAF), which is said to have saved over 90,000 lives in Somalia, now run by her two physician daughters. This organization includes a school, nutritional center, and hospital. It also provides basic necessities (i.e., shelter, water, supplies) primarily to women and children in Somalia. Thus far, it has served an estimated 2 million people. Dr. Abdi was awarded numerous honors including the Roosevelt Four Freedoms Award, Women of Impact from the WITW Foundation, nomination for the Nobel Peace Prize, and numerous others. Her biography, *Keeping Hope Alive: One Woman: 90,000 Lives Changed*, is one I recommend to any employed mother.

RECEIVING SUPPORT IN SPIRITUAL COMMUNITIES

Spiritual and religious communities are other venues for support. Connecting with employed mothers within your spiritual or religious community can increase your support during this major life transition. If a group does not exist at your particular church or organization, consider starting one. For example, if a play group is scheduled during working hours, consider coordinating a play group for a workday evening or weekend. If it does not exist, create it! It does not have to feel overwhelming or exhausting but can be as simple as a Friday Night Potluck or Weekend Meetup at a nearby park.

Another avenue of support often offered within spiritual and religious communities is pastoral

---

23   Abdi, H. (2013). *Keeping hope alive: One woman: 90,000 lives changed*. Grand Central Publishing. Clinton, H. R., & Clinton, C. (2019). *The book of gutsy women: Favorite stories of courage and resilience*. Simon & Schuster.

counseling. Even venting to a safe spiritual leader can provide validation and empathy during a time when you need it more than ever. You are worthy and deserving of support during this transition. One mother I interviewed suggested taking any pressure off yourself to attend a weekly faith service. She explained that once she gave herself permission to integrate the practice of her faith in the way that felt healthy for her (and her family), that was when she reconnected with her spirituality. Instead of pressuring her family to attend a Sunday service, for example, she found organic opportunities to integrate faith in a way that felt more meaningful: prayers at bedtime, streaming a relevant sermon from the comfort of their pajamas in the living room, or leaning upon scripture during trying times.

Shannon Bartlett, a mother you will hear from later, baptized her son in the church of her upbringing. Although she did not fully subscribe to the core beliefs of the religion, Shannon and her partner wanted to provide him with an early spiritual foundation. What Shannon did not expect was how therapeutic the parent preparation classes would be, not in terms of religious teachings but as a way to make time and space to focus on her partnership with her husband. This was something she deeply missed. During this time, they united on the spiritual goal to teach their son that he is loved unconditionally and that there is a great power out there. Her religious community was not a place she expected to find solace, but she was surprised in the way it nourished her partnership and paved the way for teaching her son unconditional love.

GEMS FROM GINA DEBENEDETTI

Gina is 38 years young and the mother of a 7-year-old daughter. Gina lives in the Greater Chicago Area, a proud member of a large, loving Italian family, notably headed by the wise Grandma Flora and Nonna Florence, matriarchs like no other. Gina is an employed mother, an Enterprise Account Manager, managing remotely as well as frequenting client sites primarily on the West Coast. Gina has worked for this same company for over 14 years, a time period represented by a spectrum of transitions: promotions, marriage, motherhood, and the Covid-19 global pandemic. Gina also struggled with infertility. Her journey to motherhood was not an easy one, relatable to so many of us.

Here is a speed-round of advice from Gina on six of the dimensions of wellness.

Emotional. Gina learned to dance through separation anxiety not without a few sprains and falls. Her work required travel to client sites, which initially resulted in separation anxiety. Gina eloquently described one particular client site visit that ended with inclement weather and subsequent flight cancellations. As her separation anxiety skyrocketed, she snapped into action, transferring airports and airlines, simply to arrive a few hours prior to the originally rescheduled flight. Looking back, it was clear to Gina that she *could* have gotten a good night's rest at a hotel and returned to her daughter the next day. Her daughter was safe. *She* was safe. Anyone experiencing separation anxiety, though, knows all too well how anxiety influences your behavior and can feel like an unrelenting drive to hold your baby in your arms. With practice, and a therapist, Gina beautifully learned to dance through this separation anxiety. She reframed her business trips from *abandoning her daughter* to *enjoyable time away*. She used these trips to focus on self-health, connect with other employed moms, and developed strategies to schedule her trips around her daughter's schedule (i.e., flight arrival early in the morning). "I learned that it's about the collective time spent with my daughter. Was I present? Was I making space for her?"

Intellectual. Gina recommends purchasing a planner and *using it!* Writing things down helped her recall important dates and became an invaluable reference tool.

Physical. Gina emphasized the importance of exercising not only for the physical but also the mental benefit. Gina suggests finding a time that works for *you*. Gina utilized her lunch break to exercise but also knew of women who exercised before the kids woke up or after they went to bed. Gina exercised in front of her daughter to model that exercise is a *good* thing. In terms of nutritious meal prepping, Gina found balance in semi-homemade meals. For example, as an Italian who loves to cook, she would purchase quality meatballs from Whole Foods that she incorporated into homemade entrees. As a quick snack, she offered the brilliant suggestion to quarter and freeze peanut butter and jelly sandwiches, so they're always ready to go.

Women can build
STABILITY.
Women can build
peace

- *Dr. Hawa Abdi*

Financial. Gina emphasized the importance of saving *early* to maximize compound interest. She also recommends delivery services for groceries and other necessities. After accounting for time and gas she would have spent, she found that it was cheaper to have someone else do it.

Occupational. *Stop* apologizing, Gina pleaded! Instead of, "I am sorry I am late," you can say, "I am here," or "Thanks for being patient," and move on. She calls women to support other women. In order to climb the ladder, women need to support one another. Set boundaries *early on*. It is hard to roll back boundaries, so set them from the start. Set a hard stop.

Social. Find allies, at work, at daycare, at the playground. Find a group of women who can relate to where you are, where you have been, and where you are going! They will come to your defense and give you the grace you need to survive this wild ride. Gina decided to create a firm boundary about having her family members serve as caregivers in order to avoid role confusion. She wanted to keep familial roles clear, and time spent with grandparents special.

"Guilt always finds a way in; Remember You Are Enough! Staying steadfast in these words is a great start in learning how to manage it."

My Pump Has Seen Some Places!
Inspired by Gina DeBenedetti

My pump has traveled with me every single place I have gone,
From Chicago's Midway Airport where I watched people pass by
To Plano and D.C. with its big windows and sunny skies!

I've pumped the whole country over while in small, cramped spaces
like The Dallas Love Airport bathroom and a stench-filled taxi in
Atlanta. While all around us traffic stopped and slowed endlessly.

Sometimes I was more comfortable, and places occasionally had
more room, Like hotels in places like Dulles and Richmond all the way
to Atlanta! Or — I'd find a quiet back corner, like at Katie's wedding
reception!

In O'Hare Airport, between watching planes and families collect piles
of patterned suitcases, I pumped in both the bathroom and the
asphalt parking lot.

The Hartsfield-Jackson and Reagan Airport bathrooms are no
different. And each can claim they got a visit from me just to pump!

When not sprawled across hotel beds or dozing in countless airports
Or trying to chase taxis down, I pump in silent, empty places.
Everywhere from Equifax offices in Alpharetta and Atlanta!

So next time you can't find me, check airport bathrooms
And the backseats of taxis and the nearest office building.
I swear I am there somewhere, just trying to find a place to pump!

"No Stage lasts forever.
The good never stays
as long as you want.
The bad doesn't leave
as fast as you hope."

—Grandma Flora—

Suggested Spiritual Reading

25 Days of Bible Verses for Mothers:
A Christian Devotional & Coloring
Journal by Shalana Frisby

This Life That is Ours: Motherhood as
Spiritual Practice by Lauren Burdette

Motherhood: A Spiritual Journey
by Ellyn Sanna

Long Days of Small Things:
Motherhood as a Spiritual Discipline
by Catherine McNiel

10 Spiritual Practices for Busy Parents
by Jacqueline Kramer

Dimension of Wellness:
Intellectual

NOTES

Notes

CHAPTER 3

INTELLECTUAL WELLNESS

THE ART AND SCIENCE OF MANAGING TIME. YOUR ONE FINITE RESOURCE.

You are juggling a hundred balls, carrying a tremendous mental load, day in and day out. For working mothers, time management takes on a whole new level. You've already achieved superstar status but get ready to add one more badge – *superior time management* – to your motherhood sash! I don't need to tell you that time management for a working mother requires that you use every possible tool – technology, list making, to-do lists, outsourcing, and beyond! – to squeeze every last drop out of every single minute. However, amidst the busyness of it all, it is also possible to do so mindfully. It *is* possible to multitask while also being grounded and present. Be patient with yourself as you find your rhythm.

That extra dose of patience is all the more needed now in a landscape altered by COVID: from heated vaccine debates playing out all around us to playdate risk assessments unfolding across our kitchen tables, the decision making is constant. Give yourself a giant pat on the back. You've done a lot. It is not easy to be constantly weighing pros and cons, evaluating new information, planning for a future that seems to be ever-more uncertain. First and foremost: brava. And, at the same time: let's recognize that everybody has a limit to their cognitive capacities; this ongoing high mental output has consequences. So if you're experiencing some brain fog or decision fatigue, number one, make sure to pay attention to those signs. Number two, ask yourself: what is healthiest for you in terms of healing after doing this for several years?

One of the biggest struggles I hear from new moms as they try to find that rhythm is how to estimate how much time a task will take. In the early days of working motherhood, running late tends to happen as a matter of course, ramping up a feeling of pressure that can make every task feel like disarming a bomb. For high-stress activities such as getting out of the house with a little one – or getting out of the house *without* a little one, while remembering all your work gear – I recommend writing down the required steps along with the average amount of time required for completion. How long does it take you to pack your pump? How long does it take you to check that your diaper bag is fully stocked? What if you have to add in a quick feed, a new diaper, or a whole outfit change? The time you allot in your head might misalign with reality. Accurately capturing the amount of time required for each task will give you a more realistic measure for time management. Providing yourself fifteen minutes of preparation when a task truly requires thirty will set you up for failure and turn you into a giant ball of stress. On the flip side, if you allot yourself thirty minutes and then finish in twenty, you can enjoy the sense of calm satisfaction when you arrive at your destination ahead of time.

Ruth Bader Ginsburg

Every time I hear or read about the late Ruth Bader Ginsburg's transition to motherhood, my eyes transform into waterfalls. Imagine the intensity of law school coursework, intensified by caring for her toddler while *simultaneously* caring for her husband undergoing cancer treatment. That cocktail of palpable stress, challenging coursework, and sleepless nights transports me to the stressful first few months of employed motherhood. During moments when time management and discipline in employed motherhood feel impossible, I turn to examples of women who model the possibility of the impossible. Who are inspirational employed mothers into whom *you* can lean when you need a dose of inspiration?

Output of Mental Energy

Employed motherhood requires us to carry an immense mental burden: work commitments, childcare coordination, lactation, medical appointments, and – and – *and*! If we are going to allow ourselves as employed mothers to thrive versus simply survive, we must develop habits and strategies to help us succeed. In order to wrap my mind around the difficulty of completing one of the hundreds of tasks or making one of the hundreds of decisions floating around in my brain, I find it helpful to think about the level of output of mental energy I give to each, according to three categories: (1) minimal, (2) moderate, and (3) high. I recommend this exercise in order to try to get as objective as possible about how much energy a certain task deserves. Sometimes we can get caught up in the moment and give too much energy to something that doesn't deserve it. Other times we might get overwhelmed by all the small things and rush through a decision that merits careful consideration.

Minimal Mental Output. The implications of these tasks and decisions are minor, posing no significant risk to yourself, your family, and/or your work commitments. Think: dinner preparation, purchasing a birthday gift for a colleague, or paying bills. These tasks might be the ideal candidate for outsourcing and delegation.

Moderate Mental Output. Tasks and decisions in this category have some importance and require action in the near future. Their implications pose some potential harm to yourself, your family, and/or your work commitments. Think: unexpected car trouble on a busy day. In addition to relying on your partner, you may be able to enlist close friends and trusted collaborators for assistance.

High Mental Output. These tasks and decisions have the most importance and/or require immediate action. There's a lot at stake here, for yourself, your family, and/or your work commitments. Think: receiving a call at work from your childcare provider that your child is running a high fever. These tasks will need to be handled by you or someone in your closest circle

If a given task is not an emergency, and you do not have the capacity at that moment to provide the proper amount of mental output to a task or decision, consider the following:

- Come back to the task at a later time when your capacity and cup is full.

- Delegate the task or decision making to your partner or trusted friend or family member.

- Break the task or decision into smaller parts and tackle some of the parts.

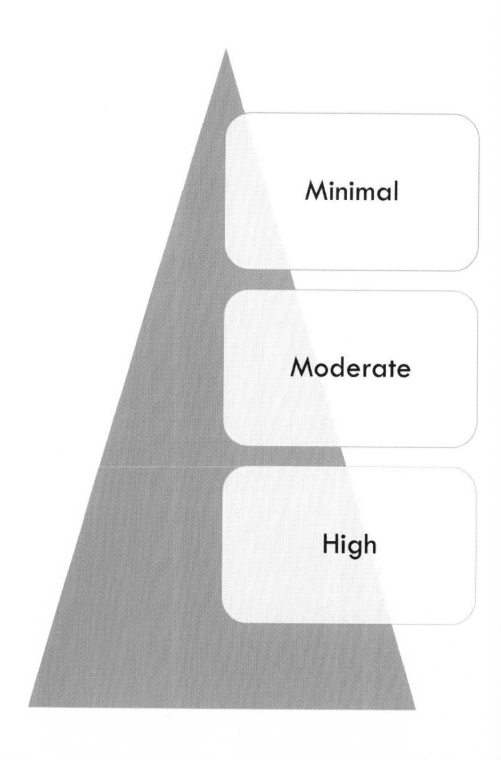

As you categorize your tasks, it may help to input them into a task management tool so they aren't endlessly circling around your head. These tools have all kinds of helpful built-in features, allowing you to set deadlines, request reminders, assign work to others, break up tasks into subtasks, indicate their level of importance and – my favorite – mark them as completed. The market for task planning software has exploded during COVID, with dozens of options, such as Google Calendar, Cozi, Notion, Trello… the list goes on (and will likely change faster than I can update this book). Pick one that works for you, or develop your own method. All that matters is that everyone who needs to use it gets – and stays – on the same page.

Mindful efficiency

There are only 24 hours in a day. Yet as a society, we've turned multitasking into a mindset that proves it *is* possible to be in more than one place at one time. The rise of video calls during the pandemic only heightened this feeling, as work-life boundaries only grew more porous.

Now, let's start from this hard truth: working moms *need* more than 24 hours in a day. The demands are infinite and, unfortunately, most of them are not opt-out-able. At the same time, no one gets a medal for burnout, and trying to earn one is just a form of self-sabotage. So while I'm *not* recommending we perpetuate the stereotype of the disheveled woman emanating frenetic energy, I also recognize it's also not realistic (or helpful) to tell working mothers to scale back on their activities to the bare essentials.

Instead, I like the concept of *mindful efficiency*: you can be present and grounded as you wait at the doctor's office while also mindfully grocery shopping on your smartphone; or while you listen to a professional podcast on your commute home. Try, whenever possible, to engage in mindful task pairing – putting together two tasks that complement one another. My favorite example is to go for a walk with a friend: you get to exercise, spend time outdoors, and strengthen social ties. Approach it as an experiment, and check in with yourself to see if the pairing was successful: Did you feel like the activities detracted from one another? If so, try a different pairing. (Is folding laundry while watching TV a great way to keep your hands busy or a way to ruin your favorite show?)

The key to practicing mindful efficiency is to keep yourself centered on your "why." If you keep focused on your core values – to maximize the amount of quality time spent with those who matter most to you and to make an impact at work – you'll feel internally motivated to integrate efficient practices into everyday life. Your mindset will also contribute to your ability to practice mindful efficiency. When you transition from one task to the next, envision yourself dancing. It does *not* have to feel like a jerk or sudden stop on a rollercoaster. Take a deep breath and mindfully transition to a new task as if gracefully dancing.

Your future self will thank you. Imagine five extra minutes spent on the floor savoring baby giggles and encouraging your little one to master a milestone. Those five minutes saved from earlier in the day will pay off tenfold.

Suggestions for mindful efficiency:

In general, limit distractions, combine physical and mental activities, stay organized (you do not have time to spend searching for items around your house), and commit to self-discipline (concentration buys time)!

- Hands-free pumping (find an exceptional pumping bra)

- Process a complex work issue in the shower or during your workout routine

- Use your lunch break to recharge and gain some headspace

- Prepare multiple dinners at once, on the weekends or days off

- Listen to a work-related podcast on your commute

Listing

Once you have entered motherhood, you now fully understand the coined term, "mom brain" and "momnesia"! Between sleep deprivation and hormonal changes, your memory is just not what it was before having children. To complicate things, add in employment! Writing lists will truly serve as a second brain to help you remember all of the important tasks that need attention and completion. For me, it also felt cathartic to check something off my list. Some days, I would look around and wonder, "What did I even accomplish?" Looking back on a tangible list can serve as a reminder that you accomplished *a lot.*

My partner and I shared a list, which we both updated throughout the day, via a smartphone app. This strengthened our partnership – we needed each other more than ever to care for our children as we both worked full-time. As an exercise, sit down with your partner and identify specific categories. You can then utilize these categories on the application as separate running lists. My husband and I used a project management tool that I honestly believe saved our marriage! We could review and update anytime, anywhere, via our phones, tablets, or computers – and we could do it asynchronously, which meant we didn't have to spend our limited one-on-one time handling household admin. What we also found helpful was sub-tasking: breaking a bigger task into multiple steps. I remember one specific instance where my partner had added an important document needed for a medical appointment requiring several sub-tasks to obtain. It was a lifesaver as I received reminder notices and could review specific notes about the needed documents.

Outsource if Feasible

I often hear employed mothers provide long-winded explanations to why they simply cannot outsource. I'm here to tell you, "When possible, outsource." Employed motherhood is stressful, exhausting, and demanding. You *can* and *should* take tasks off your plate. Ultimately, time is our one absolutely finite resource. Why not spend your precious time leaning into those you love?

Examples of outsourcing:

- House cleaning (even if once per month for deep cleaning)
- Organization services / assistants (one-time or on-going)
- As-needed personal assistants
- Laundry services
- Dog walking
- Landscaping (even seasonally)
- Childcare (daycare, weekend sitter, au pair)
- Grocery shopping
- Cooking (meal kit, takeout, delivery)
- Birthday parties

One of the ripple effects of covid on economy is that there are more options than ever, for these kinds of low-commitment, outsourced services. Give one a try and, if it doesn't work, no big loss!

WORKING HAS COGNITIVE BENEFITS

I know, firsthand, how difficult it is to identify cognitive benefits of working amidst the exhaustion, mom brain, and cognitive postpartum fog. There *are* cognitive benefits to employed motherhood. Open yourself to moments when you can acknowledge the cognitive benefits of being back at work. Shortly after returning to work after giving birth to my second daughter, I had completely forgotten how to conduct a basic mental status exam. This was wildly concerning as I worked in an emergency setting – fast paced with high-risk patients. Consumed by panic, I reviewed one of my manuals and by no short of a miracle, I regained the fundamentals of the evaluation.

I wonder, if I had not returned to work, how much of my clinical evaluation would have been lost. Not to any fault of my own, but simply due to physiological changes to my body and not having practiced this skill for nearly four months. This stopped me in my tracks. I paused and for the first time realized how much physiological change my body went through during the postpartum process. I share this to encourage you to stop and take pause. You underwent ten months of pregnancy, birthed a child, and underwent even more changes as your postpartum body acclimated. It is *okay* – it is *healthy* – to acknowledge a cognitive change, and subsequently, offer your body some patience and grace as it regains those cognitive functions essential for your job functioning.

Maintain and Expand Competency

I hear many women express their fear that they are returning to work as *less than*. "I'm *just* a tired mom" or "I have no brain cells left." I get it. I really do. *But* consider the wisdom you have to offer as a mother: the wisdom from having undergone childbirth and a major life transition. No doubt you have the superpowers such as time management, prioritization, and multitasking. These skills matter, and your contribution is valuable. Do *not* let anyone tell you otherwise. The wisdom you bring to that workplace is greater than any conference, training, or degree. Categorically.

Remaining in the workforce can provide opportunities to maintain and expand your competency, for example by practicing skills when most fields are evolving. When you leave the field for a short period of time such as your parental leave, you might be surprised how much your field changes in just a few weeks or months. Remind yourself that maintaining competency is a benefit, particularly on hard days when you want nothing more than to put in your two weeks' notice.

You can also expand your competency and skills in your professional field by attending conferences, trainings, and ongoing consultation with peers and colleagues. These are often paid for by employers or tax deductible. When I attended overnight conferences, I built in "me time" as I knew this was a rare opportunity to enjoy a full night's rest or enjoy a long, multicourse dinner sans child. I always returned intellectually, physically, and socially rejuvenated.

Did you know?

THERE ARE FOODS THAT BOOST YOUR BRAIN!

Harvard Health researched the best brain foods:

Green, leafy vegetables	Rich in brain-healthy nutrients like Vitamin K, lutein, folate, and beta carotene.	Sources include: kale, spinach, greens (collard, mustard, radish, turnip, beet, dandelion), swiss chard, arugula
Berries	Flavonoids, the natural plant pigments that give berries their brilliant hues, may also help improve memory.	Sources include: blackberries, raspberries, strawberries, blueberries, cranberries, elderberries, goji, acai
Tea and Coffee	The caffeine in your morning cup of coffee or tea might offer more than just a short-term concentration boost. Caffeine might also help solidify new memories. Now you have an excuse to stop for coffee on your way to the office! You're welcome.	Sources include: black tea, green tea (including matcha), white tea, oolong, and coffee
Walnuts	Nuts are excellent sources of protein and healthy fats, and walnuts in particular might also improve memory. A 2015 study from UCLA linked higher walnut consumption to improved cognitive test scores.	Look for walnuts, but some other healthful nuts include almonds, pistachios and cashews

Dimension of Wellness: Physical

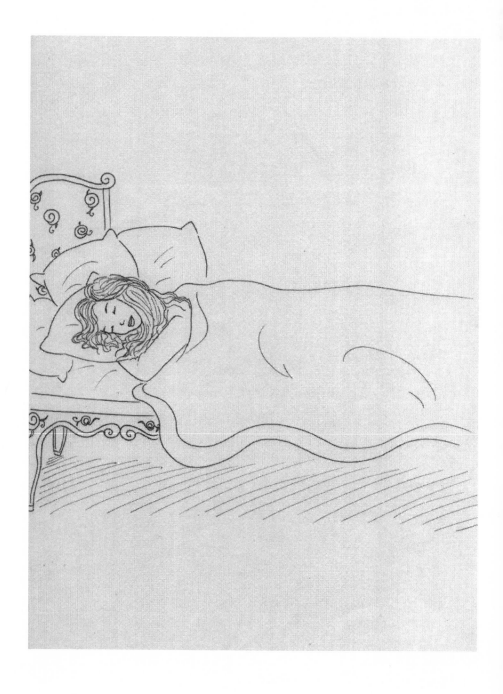

NOTES

_____

_____

_____

_____

_____

_____

_____

_____

_____

_____

_____

_____

_____

_____

_____

_____

_____

CHAPTER 4

PHYSICAL WELLNESS

I n the early perinatal period, our attention goes – rightly – to attending to the physical needs of our new baby. We document wet and dirty diapers, measure ounces of milk, chart inches and pounds added to their growing body. It might feel inevitable that our own wellbeing slips into the background, but all the cliches are there for a reason: *you can't pour from an empty cup, you have to put your own oxygen mask on before helping those around you*... It's all true.

That doesn't mean it's easy. As I walk you through the dimensions of physical wellness a working mother needs to develop and preserve, I recognize that there will be competing and conflicting needs – not just with your new baby, but every other member of your household: other children, relatives, pets (who might be demanding walks at inconvenient times) and, if you have one, your partner.

It's a balancing act, to be sure, and at the center of it is the most magical of all medicines: sleep.

PRESERVE AND PROTECT YOUR SLEEP. MAGICAL MEDICINE.

I know my audience, so I say this with the utmost sensitivity – *rest*. Preserve and protect your sleep. High quality sleep can serve as a protective factor from a variety of disorders. For example, one study revealed that although sleep problems significantly improved from six weeks to seven months postpartum, linear regression analyses indicated that women who experienced worsening or minimal improvement of sleep problems faced higher depressive symptoms at seven months postpartum.[24]

- Are you having difficulty falling asleep?

- Are you having difficulty maintaining sleep?

- Are you tired despite having slept at least seven to eight hours of sleep?

If you answered yes to any of the following, consult with your OB/GYN or Primary Care Physician to address a sleep disturbance.

Some tips for sleep hygiene include:

1. avoid stimulants (i.e., caffeine) close to bedtime

2. if possible (and cleared by OB/GYN), move your body throughout the day

3. avoid foods or drinks that could disrupt sleep such as alcohol and sugary, fried, or spicy foods

---

24   Lewis, B. A., Gjerdingen, D., Schuver, K., Avery, M., & Marcus, B. H. (2018). The effect of sleep pattern changes on postpartum depressive symptoms. *BMC Women's Health, 18*(1), 1–7. https://doi.org/10.1186/s12905-017-0496-6

4. establish a consistent bedtime routine (stretching, bubble bath, reading, prayer/meditation)

5. create a relaxing, pleasant sleep environment (temperature of room, level of darkness, comfort or blankets/pillows, white noise).

Make a sleep plan, in advance of your return to work

In a household with a newborn, making sure everyone is getting enough sleep can feel like a game of Twister. When you return to the workforce after parental leave, make sleep – yours, your baby's and the rest of your family's – the centerpiece of the conversation.

- Be mindful about stress around baby's sleep and how that might be impacting your overall mood.

- Consider how you and your partner plan to handle night-time awakenings, feedings, etc. If you've been taking on the lion's share during your leave, now is a time to look at your work schedules and decide what needs to be altered.

- Some people find it helpful to bring in a sleep consultant (often with a considerable price tag). If you want to go this route, ideally look to schedule the service before your return to work.

Rejuvenate on the Weekends

Whenever possible, refrain from overcommitting yourself on the weekends, particularly in the beginning phase of your transition back to work. I often tell clients: rest *is* productivity. My partner and I "split the weekends" so he covered the children on Saturday mornings while I slept in and I covered the children on Sunday mornings while he slept in. That way, we knew that we could depend on a replenishment of sleep at least one night per week. I also found a deep appreciation for our partnership and ability to care for one another (and the kids) in this way.

Another shift in my behavior was slowing down. After living through the go-go-go of the work week, I found myself entering the weekends with that same energy and pacing. On Friday nights, I intentionally set various reminders – mostly visual cues – to prompt me to *slow down*. This promoted more mindful interactions with my little ones and oh how we savored the weekends.

Hire a Night Nanny

Night nannies' primary purpose is to care for infants so the parents can rest. Some duties include feeding babies, changing diapers, swaddling, soothing, and bringing the baby to the mother to nurse. Sleep is a protective factor for perinatal mood and anxiety disorders (PMADS). Some additional benefits of maintaining adequate sleep include improved work performance and productivity and higher quality parent-child interactions.

The obvious downside to hiring a night nanny (or doula/NCS) is the cost. If the cost is an issue for you, consider hiring a night nanny a few days per week instead of full-time. *Or* hire a night nanny one time per week or month. This way you can count a good night's rest at least once in a while. Strategically schedule them on nights before an important work presentation or later in the week when you could benefit from a full night's rest. Another idea is to have a family member commit to one night per month to cover a night shift. This might supplement or replace the paid support.

FUEL YOUR BODY WITH HEALTHY FOOD

You will need stamina to sustain yourself during this strenuous life transition, which means fueling your body with healthy food. Focus on a balanced diet consisting of vegetables, fruits, grains, protein, and dairy. In order to ensure you have a balanced lunch to get yourself through a full day at work, consider packing your lunch the night before to ensure you balance each category. I bought a few lunch containers with several separate compartments, which served as reminders that each one should be filled with different food categories. For example, one sample container had blueberries (fruit), cottage cheese (dairy/protein), carrots (vegetable), and whole grain crackers (grain). Another sample container had bananas and cashew butter (fruit/healthy fat), red peppers (vegetable), whole milk yogurt (dairy), and brown rice (grain). These multi-compartmental lunches, based on unprocessed foods, are simple to assemble. I was able to snack all day, which helped with lactation, and allowed me to take smaller breaks versus a long lunch. Whatever your approach, as long as you focus on a balanced diet, find a system that works best for your routine and lifestyle.

An essential part of balanced eating is *hydration*. Drink copious amounts of water, especially if you are lactating. Mayo Clinic recommends about 11.5 cups of fluids per day for women. This should be adjusted based on your exercise level, the climate in which you live, your overall health, and pregnancy/lactation. A good indication that your fluid intake is adequate is (1) you rarely feel thirsty and (2) your urine is light yellow or clear. Clear pee is the way to be!

*Nourishing Newborn Mothers: Ayurvedic Recipes
to Heal your Mind, Body and Soul after Childbirth
by Julia Jones*

Deepti Arora, IBCLC CPFE IYCF Specialist and Author of *MamaMade Recipes*, developed some recipes to support you in your transition to employed motherhood.

All the recipes are made with whole ingredients, offering a rich source of nutrition after birth. They aid in digestion, healing, and increased milk production.

Cumin & Fennel Tea

2 – 4 Servings

Boil a quart of water with 2 TBSP of cumin seeds and 2 TBSP of fennel seeds. Strain and sip warm or hot throughout the day. If your baby was born in the summer, let the tea cool then sip throughout the day but do not refrigerate. You can make a batch of warm tea each morning and sip while you work.

Nourishing Dal

Ingredients

- 3 tsp olive oil, ghee, coconut oil

- 2 tsp cumin seeds

- 2 tsp mustard seeds

- 2 pinches of ground turmeric

- 3 cups of red lentils, rinsed

- lemon juice and salt

- chopped cilantro

Instructions

1. Heat the olive oil in a large saucepan over medium heat. Add the mustard seeds, cumin seeds, and turmeric. Sauté for 2–3 minutes, until fragrant.

2. Rinse the lentils.

3. Add 6 cups of water to the saucepan and stir.

4. Bring to a boil, then reduce the heat to low and simmer until tender for about 15 minutes.

5. Garnish with lemon juice, extra olive oil or ghee, and cilantro.

6. Enjoy with your favorite grain.

Cashew & Chia Milkshake

Ingredients

- 4 cups raw or dry roasted cashews, unsalted

- 3 fresh dates, seed removed

- 2 tsp ground cinnamon

- 2 tsp vanilla extract

- ¼ cup chia seeds

Instructions

1. Put everything in a blender.

2. Add 7 cups of water.

3. Blend until the milk is frothy, 2–3 minutes.

4. Strain the milk in a nut bag or a mesh strainer.

5. Serve immediately.

MEAL EFFICIENCY

You are busy. You are tired. Efficiency is the name of the game. When considering meal preparation, remember to (1) keep it simple and (2) fuel your body with healthy food. This is also a great opportunity to incorporate your partner. For breakfast, my partner and I took turns making morning coffee. We simplified the process by purchasing a simple coffee pot, no more than $30. We prepped the coffee pot the evening prior, which only required the simple press of a button to start the coffee to brew. Because of my morning time constraints of completing my own routine and preparing for daycare, I relied on on-the-go breakfasts such as a banana/breakfast bar and yogurt/granola. On Sunday nights, my partner and I often froze breakfast burritos and egg bites to quickly microwave for our morning commutes. We also purchased reusable coffee mugs that were environmentally friendly and, bonus, kept our coffee very, very hot for times when we were distracted or interrupted.

> **Gluten Free Protein Balls**
>
> Ingredients:
>
> *1/2 cup peanut butter (you can replace with any type of nut or seed butter)*
> *1 cup gf rolled oats*
> *1/2 ground flaxseed*
> *1 tsp chia seeds*
> *1/4 cup organic, pure maple syrup (or honey!)*
> *1/3 cup chocolate chips*

Simplifying dinner preparation allows for less stress and more quality time in the evenings with those you love most. This was my motivation to nourish each dimension of wellness. My partner and I divided and conquered dinner preparation. I cooked on Mondays and Wednesdays; he cooked on Tuesdays and Thursdays. On Fridays we ate out or ordered takeout and on the weekends we either ate out or cooked together. Whoever did not cook was in charge of cleanup. To simplify meals, I focused on a protein (chicken, fish), vegetable, and a healthy grain. When using a crock pot or Instapot, I doubled recipes for leftovers to take for next-day lunches. I also found that soups make for excellent next-day lunches. Give yourself permission to simplify and spend less time preparing/cooking dinner.

Additional Meal Efficiency Tips

1. Consider a **meal-kit delivery**. On Saturdays, we established a ritual of making the meal-kit together. It *almost* felt like date night again.

2. If someone asks how they can help, **ask for a few meals**. "We are covered with childcare, but we sure could use some frozen dinners!" (There were a few times when I nearly slipped in, "Oh, and a Starbucks gift card!")

3. **Take out or delivery**. We utilized this option more than I would like to admit, especially the first few weeks of my return to work. One of the positive developments of the post-COVID world is that many local caterers and restaurants have started to specialize in healthy family-style meals, meant to be eaten over the course of a week.

4. **Meal prep on the weekends.** Alternatively, double recipes you make during the week and freeze the other half.

5. For mornings, **prepare your coffee pot the night before or automate your brew**.

Quick breakfast ideas – 2 minutes or less

Mash ½ banana and mix in one egg. Sprinkle in cinnamon. Microwave for 1 minute. Stir.

Microwave for an additional minute. Top with any type of nut or seed butter. This breakfast is packed with healthy carbohydrates, protein, and fats.

Purchase your favorite protein bars. (Check the nutrition label to make sure it has a fair amount of protein, compared to sugars and fats, and includes whole food ingredients. RxBar and some forms of Kind Bars are good choices.) On rushed mornings, these can be lifesaving. I also kept a few in my car for "those" mornings.

Create your own morning trail mix. I created a morning trail mix with mixed nuts and seeds (I preferred pumpkin seeds and cashews), dried berries (mulberries and goji berries, both superfoods), and some type of sweetness such as coconut, figs, or dates.

I supplemented my coffee with plant-based oils (MCT oil, for example) and creamers for additional energy.

A few examples of quick, simple meals:

*   Chicken, broccoli, and brown rice in an instapot. Add herbs and seasonings of your choice. Preparation and cook time < 15 minutes.

*   Grilled salmon (I used a grill pan) with peas (yes, frozen), and whole grain toast. Preparation and cooking < 20 minutes.

> Recipe book suggestion:
> *The Working Mother Cookbook: Fast, Easy Recipes from the Editors of Working Mother Magazine*

MOVE YOUR BODY

The American College of Obstetricians and Gynecologists outlines multiple benefits to body movements in the postpartum period. Once cleared by your OB/GYN, enjoy the benefits of exercise such as muscle strength, increased energy, potential protection from postpartum depression, promotion of better sleep, stress relief, and weight loss. Employed mothers should reap these same benefits.

However, given the time constraints and increased competing demands at home and work, you might need to reconceptualize *how* you move your body. Body movement does *not* have to look like a 2-hour bootcamp or 90-minute hot yoga session (although if this is an option for you, you go, mama!). I encourage mothers transitioning to employed motherhood to reconceptualize body movement from extensive blocks of intense workout sessions to manageable, pragmatic segments integrated throughout your workday.

Don't think of this as a watered-down approach to fitness. Recent research confirms the significant benefits of this "snack" method – especially for people whose jobs require long seated hours.[25] An exercise snack could look like going up and down several flights of stairs a few times per day, an intense, ten-minute bike ride, or even running in place next to your desk.

Move your body
to show your
body LOVE,
not PUNISHMENT

25   Moore, D. R., Williamson, E. P., Hodson, N., Estafanos, S., Mazzulla, M., Kumbhare, D., & Gillen, J. B. (2022). Walking or body weight squat "activity snacks" increase dietary amino acid utilization for myofibrillar protein synthesis during prolonged sitting. *Journal of Applied Physiology, 133*(3), 777–785. https://doi.org/10.1152/japplphysiol.00106.2022

Some ways to integrate body movement into your workday:

- Take the stairs instead of the elevator

- Exercise rituals (also known as 'habit stacking', i.e., five squats every time you use the restroom)

- Walk during breaks

- Use a standing desk

- Buy a walking pad for use during audio calls or during breaks

- Park a block over to increase your steps

- Stretch before and/or after pumping

- Take advantage of a workplace gym, if available

- Set up a simple fitness area in your home, for quick exercise snacks (as small as a yoga mat!)

WHAT TO WEAR. YOUR WORKPLACE WARDROBE.

Your body created life. Your hips are wider, your skin might be stretched with battle scars, and perhaps you are lactating. Many women return to work with engorged breasts, cesarean or tearing scars still healing, and lingering pregnancy weight. Your body has undergone tremendous change, and it deserves patience as it acclimates postpartum. As you return to work, allow yourself to find clothes you feel comfortable and confident in. Offer your body some compassion as it continues to heal. Hello knit, spandex, and elastic!

Clothing

Undergarments. Focus on comfort and functionality. If lactating, consider a comfortable nursing bra that is easy to maneuver when you pump. Not all nursing and pumping bras are created equal. Shop around. You deserve to feel comfortable in your undergarments. It will be worth the time and financial investment. Purchase a few different colors in order to pair with tops. If lactating, try on bras and see how they feel and look with breast pads. Do they become lumpy? Are the breast pads secure? At the very least, buy yourself some new, fresh underwear before your transition back to work! A lot of brands now offer underwear with built-in liners, which can help minimize worries about any fluid leaks.

Tops. For most moms returning to work, tops are transitional. Think loose and stretchy! I did not spend the time or money on *must have* tops, as I knew these would head right into the trash after I finished lactating and my boobs deflated. This also removed the pressure of rushing my postpartum body. Instead, I focused on finding milk-friendly colors in case of a spill or leak. It only took one spill on a green cotton shirt to take note *never* to wear that color again. If pumping, consider tops that will cooperate with a breast pump. I found button-down or half-button-down tops particularly pump friendly. Nursing and maternity tops might also work for you. Keep in mind that your nipples might harden or protrude after pumping. Wait a few minutes after pumping before interacting in-person with colleagues. If you are in a time crunch, bring a shawl or large sweater if that would help you feel more comfortable. Find what works for *you*.

Pants. Fitting into my pre-baby work pants on my first day back was laughable. Nope, not happening. My pant legs fit, but my uterus was ever-so-ballooned, impossible to zip and button. If you can zip up your pants all the way, awesome (seriously!), but if not, it is *okay*. I relied on my maternity pants until I was able to return to my pre-baby pants, which happened *several* months after returning to work. Another option is to shop for some new or secondhand pants in a size that feels comfortable. I utilized second-hand and thrift stores for transitional items, keeping an eye out for pants with pockets to carry small emergency items like hair ties and breast pads.

For work-from-home moms, you've got license to be as comfy as you possibly can manage. Athleisure bottoms can be your new uniform. It's a true perk of remote work, so enjoy it.

Shoes. Your body has undergone tremendous change. Like many mothers, your joints have been impacted. Perhaps you have experienced back pain, and your skeletal system is still adjusting to weight fluctuations, childbirth, hormones, and beyond. To ease discomfort and support your body's realignment, start with your feet. Purchase comfortable, functional shoes to bolster your healing. There are many brands designed for comfort *and* style. Take some time to research comfort-oriented brands that fit your style. Your future self will thank you for it.

Makeup routine. Whatever your routine looks like, if you wear makeup to work, create a five-minute routine for *those* mornings when you are running against the clock. One strategy would be to leave a small makeup bag in the glove department for emergency mornings. You know, the ones when your waterfall of tears causes mascara to paint your already swollen eye bags, or when you realize that you got interrupted before completing both of your eyes. Whatever the reason, equip yourself in advance so you have one less crisis to mitigate.

Clothing to avoid. Those high-cut nursing and pumping bras are just not made for low-cut shirts. Also, you know those dresses hiding in your closet only accessible from the back zipper? *Not* the time to pull those out. Trying to maneuver a pumping session in one of those or attempting to take it off following a long workday will only lead to frustration, and maybe a dance with scissors. Avoid anything with cling. You might get some confused looks when a misshapen breast pad becomes the centerpiece to your ensemble. Speaking of those lovely breast pads, in the case that your milk leaks beyond your pad, avoid solid blouses, which tend to show milk leaks more than patterns. I purchased several patterned blouses at discounted and secondhand stores, knowing I would be throwing them away once I fully weaned. For the finale, avoid *anything* that is uncomfortable. Apply this to all apparel, not just the basics. Life is too short to spend the day uncomfortable. You do *not* have to suffer through one more thing. Dress comfortably.

Accessories

Between the importance of hydration, postpartum hair loss, and the unpredictability of your first postpartum menstruation, you will be glad if you prepare accordingly. Some accessories to purchase prior to your first day back at work include: a reliable water bottle, extra makeup, lint roller, hair ties/clips, breast pads, tampons or pads, and a transport bag. Staying hydrated can be much easier with a functional water bottle. A personal ongoing battle for me was keeping track of my keys. I purchased a key finder and attached a bright lanyard to my keychain, which saved countless hours of searching.

Water bottles. Some considerations when purchasing a water bottle include (1) leakage potential, (2) whether it's baby proof and safe (absent of small parts), (3) sizing, and (4) is it easy to clean? Once you find the right water bottle for *you*, purchase multiple so you have an extra in case one breaks, or you are too tired to clean it for the next day. You can use the spare that is already clean.

Makeup. Keeping extra makeup in your office desk drawer can come in handy during days when hormone fluctuations result in the inevitable waterfall of tears.

Eyewear. It is not uncommon to have a postpartum prescription change, often for the better. My optometrist advised that I wait until I had fully weaned to schedule an eye examination. My current prescription was still active so I purchased two additional pairs of glasses that could withstand slobber, unexpected overextensions, and use as teethers. One of the best postpartum purchases I ever made. For work-from-home moms or moms who do a lot of online calls, anti-reflective coating on your lenses is helpful to reduce camera glare.

Lint roller and hair ties/clips. When postpartum hair loss comes full force, keep a lint roller, hair ties, and clips nearby. I found it helpful to occasionally check shoulders to knees for dandruff and stray hair. You can discreetly store a mini lint roller in your desk or purse. If your hair loss is particularly intense, consider pulling your hair up in a bun or ponytail to prevent excessive hair on your work attire. Professional hair clips can provide a sleeker look on days you need to have your hair up but also need a more formal look. For work from home moms who might be called into spontaneous meetings, or take a quick shower or a nursing session between meetings – a hair tie on your desk is a true must, allowing you to quickly get yourself camera-ready (in a very basic way).

Breast pads. If lactating, keep extra breast pads in your purse, office desk, pump bag, etc. It is easy to forget to change your breast pads, and before you know it, you will start smelling like breast milk or notice a leak on your blouse. It is also important to maintain good breast hygiene to prevent thrush or other fungal or bacterial infections. I established a routine of changing my breast pads each time I used the restroom and after pumping.

Tampons or pads. That pesky first postpartum menstruation can appear at the most inconvenient of times. Prepare ahead to prevent having to panic when it comes. I did not expect my first postpartum period to come as early as it did, and although I had stashed a couple tampons in my desk, I had underestimated how heavy it would be. I also underestimated the intensity of hormones. Thank goodness for tissues. Another possible solution is to invest in underwear with built-in liners that can withstand menstrual blood or bladder leaks. This technology has come a long way, and the underwear looks and feels like a normal pair while providing peace of mind. Having a few resealable plastic baggies in your desk drawer, along with a change of underwear, can be helpful if you need to freshen up during the day.

Transport bag. Despite being a self-proclaimed minimalist – as much you can be with a child – I found towing *all the things* to-and-from the office. Keeping a transport bag in your car can be an efficient and environmentally friendly way to transport all of the items you need to carry to-and-from your office. Separating work items from motherhood items can also increase efficiency when sorting items between transports. For example, when I brought daycare forms to the office to complete during my lunch break, I knew to put them in my transport versus my work purse to help with sorting when I returned home.

When choosing the bag, what it came down to for me:

1. Is the bag washable?

2. Can the color of the bag hide spilt breast milk or baby food?

3. Is it affordable?

4. Is its sizing functional?

5. Does it have at least one zipper pocket to contain small parts?

PUMPING IN THE WORKPLACE

There's no way to sugar-coat this: Pumping in the workplace is no fun. But that doesn't mean it will always feel as confusing, chaotic and stressful as it does in the first few days.

For mamas who are learning to pump for the first time precisely as you make the transition back to work – give yourself some extra support and patience. Pumping is a challenging activity even in ideal circumstances; now add the complications of being in a semi-public or public space, with your professional obligations often in tension (if not outright conflict) with your bodily needs. It's a lot!

With work-from-home and hybrid setups becoming more common, you might have different options to negotiate – and a different pumping schedule to navigate.

Things to think about:

- How much time are you allotted for a pump break? There are workplace standards, but if your workflow doesn't allow for that, how will you handle it?

- Can you set your availability to ensure breaks between meetings? If you have regular video calls, can you pump on video – and how will you address that with clients, supervisors and co-workers?

- How easy to access is your milk storage refrigerator? Can you keep a small cooler or minifridge near your pumping area? Or is there an office fridge that's nearby?

- How easy is it to clean your pump during work? Do you need to bring plastic bags to toss the pump parts temporarily, and then plan to sterilize them later? (Don't forget a small towel as well.)

- What do you need to do physically, professionally, environmentally, psychologically and emotionally to transition yourself in and out of pumping? (I'll discuss some of the possibilities below.)

Pumping Space

Consider the setup. A little bit of time spent creating a peaceful pumping space can pay off, quite literally in liquid gold. If you need to scramble to transform your workspace every time you need to pump, you'll end up wasting time. Not to mention the fact that your environment can impact your mood and even your let down response and milk supply. You'll need to balance functionality with aesthetics, within whatever physical constraints your space might have. When I initially set up my pumping space, I thoughtfully created an aesthetically pleasing space with a picture of my daughter taped to my desk just right of where my pump would go. However, when I went to sit down for my first trial pumping session, I realized that I had not considered the placement of the outlet. Mom brain at its finest. I found a solution, but the moral of the story? Consider the setup of your pumping space and plan a trial run to work out any kinks. Pumping is the pits, so create a space that feels comfortable and functional.

Privacy. The last thing you want is for a lovely colleague to intrude while pumping. I worked in an Emergency Department, which was fast-paced and an environment where offices were frequently shared. Off the top of my head, I can recall two walk-ins. Mortifying. Learn from my shortcomings (and sleep deprivation) and create signs (or have your partner create them) for your office door. If you have any glass on the side(s) of your door, cover them up. Utilize a noise machine if you do not want passersby to hear the joyful sound of a breast pump.

Pumping in a lactation room. If you do not have a private office space in which to pump, you'll need to speak to your HR about lactation room options. (See Chapter 7 for more on federal protections surrounding workplace pumping.) Ideally, the room will be outfitted for your comfort, but if it's missing the basics – like a footstool and comfy seating – speak up and find out if

it's possible to have those items purchased. When pumping in a lactation room, you'll have to transport all your gear with you, so investing in a spacious, well-designed bag will be key. You can always bring comforting items, such as a small, framed photo of your child, to set out on the counter to look at while pumping. Other little touches that might make you feel at home could include a curated playlist and earbuds or your favorite essential oil.

Pumping breaks. Pumping at work is super exciting, no? There are, however, some tips and tricks (as also outlined above) to make your pumping experience a little less sucky. Try to keep a consistent schedule. This will serve as a cue to you, possibly others if needed, that you are taking time to pump. Veering from the schedule should be the exception not the rule. Honor yourself and pump when you have designated pump times. Do not wait until the point of engorgement to stop what you are doing to pump. When I planned my pump breaks, I scheduled them so that I ended the day ready for an enjoyable routine: nursing my daughter upon reunion at daycare. My daughter's daycare provider knew to hold off (if feasible) on her late afternoon feeding, and I would nurse her in a rocking chair at daycare. This made for a peaceful, connecting reunion.

Pumping on video calls. Wow, welcome to the 2020s! Pumping on a video call might have seemed unfathomable in 2019, now it's more common than you might think: When you've got back-to-back calls, team meetings to attend, meetings that run late – pumping on a call may be the best possible choice.

Whether you feel comfortable doing this – and how – will be a highly personal decision. You might worry the sound of the pump will make people uncomfortable, but at the same time, if you need to be an active part of the conversation, muting yourself isn't practical. (They'll get used to it!) You might worry that some people think this is unprofessional; but know that a lot of people will also see you as a super mom who is attending to multiple needs with grace.

One way to approach this is to prepare an easy statement to make at the start of the meeting, that factually describes what they should expect: "In about 15 minutes, I'll be pumping. You'll hear a low noise in the background while I'm doing this. I'll be carrying on normally, and everyone should do the same." (If you have regular meetings with the same people, you'll only have to do this once per group! It does get easier, I promise…)

Cleaning a milk pump at work. If you need to pump multiple times during the workday, you'll also need to make sure your pump parts are sanitized in boiling water. I recommend purchasing a large electric tea kettle so you can submerge the individual pump parts for about ten minutes, after first rinsing them with running tap water. Then place the sanitized parts on a dish towel to allow them to dry before returning them to their storage.

Milk Storage

Milk storage is both an art and a science. Experiment, beginning to end, using different storage containers to find your preference. I preferred smaller tubes because I found them easier to fill and label. Figure out – before your first day back – where you will store your milk. The last thing you want to navigate on your first day back is how to discreetly store your milk in a shared work fridge. If you have a private office or personal space, consider purchasing a small fridge. There are numerous brands of breast milk storage bags with built-in ice packs, which is also an option for milk storage. I kept a sharpie nearby for writing down the date and any specific contents such as caffeine or dairy. I also set a reminder on my phone for five minutes prior to the end of my workday, telling me to grab my milk. On days I forgot, I ended up texting my coworker to put my milk in the freezer – less than ideal but it got the job done.

Pumping and Wardrobe

We have already reviewed wardrobe tips and tricks, but as an additional consideration, if you need to work through your pumping break – for whatever reason – store a hands-free pumping bra in your office or pumping bag. Be kind to yourself. Do not let yourself become so engorged due to work stress that you only stop to pump when you are absolutely uncomfortable and engorged.

Pumping While Traveling for Work

Airplanes. If you need to travel via airplane for work and are lactating, this section is for you. The good news is that TSA considers breast milk in the same category as liquid medicine. Therefore, it is not subject to the three-ounce rule and also allows you to bring ice packs, empty bottles, etc. Be prepared, though, that TSA might perform screenings akin to those for other explosive screenings (this might involve opening containers). My advice is to separate your breast milk and accompanying supplies (pump, sanitation wipes, storage bags, etc.) so you can easily declare them at security. Although there is no limit to the quantity of breast milk you can bring in your carry-on, TSA encourages travelers to only bring as much breast milk, juice, or formula needed to reach their destination.

> *You can contact TSA directly at 1-866-289-9673 if you experience any issue or believe you are being misinformed by TSA personnel.*

For safety purposes, TSA will not allow women to pump while sitting on a "jump" seat (also referred to as the exit row), so plan accordingly. You also have the option of pumping in the bathroom. Spare yourself the added stress by bringing an efficient pump that you are familiar with. When I needed to pump on airplanes, I brought a manual pump that I could discreetly pump under my oversized cardigan. This way, I did not have to stress about having an outlet. Whatever works for you, do what makes you feel most comfortable. If you do bring a powered pump, check that you will have access to an outlet or bring batteries. Pack a sealable plastic bag to store your used pump parts. This way, you can easily clean them when you have the opportunity. Bring a storage container with a cooler for your milk. If needed, you can always ask a flight attendant for ice. If you do not need the milk and are pumping for milk maintenance or engorgement, feel free to dispose of the milk in the bathroom. In other words, pump and dump. Once you have finished pumping and stored your milk, be sure to applaud yourself. You just accomplished an incredible task – pumping on an airplane. Go you!

Cars. In addition to pumping on an airplane for work-related travel, it is also possible that you will need to pump in your car when driving is required for work travel. First and foremost, figure out whatever sequence works best for you. Do *you*. Below I outline a guide for successful car pumping.

Step 1: Assess your space. Are all of the wires clear and safe? Are the cup holders empty and ready to hold your bottles?

Step 2: Open your shirt and expose your hands-free bra.

Step 3: Secure your seatbelt *before* attaching to your pump. This way your seatbelt won't interfere with your pump parts. Safety first!

Step 4: Plug in your pump. Figure out the outlet prior to your first car pump experience. I used an adapter, but a battery pack is also an option.

Step 5: Attach your shields and tubes.

Step 6: Start pumping, mama!

Step 7: Enjoy the drive and some good music, a podcast, or audiobook. You are a superhuman, driving while pumping milk! Celebrate your badassery!

Step 8: Once you have arrived in a safe parking lot or a secure area, disconnect – carefully. Yes, I have cried over spilled milk. Be careful as you remove your parts. Secure your milk and place it in a cooler. You are a master multitasker!

EVER-CHANGING HORMONES

As I immersed myself in literature on hormonal changes during the perinatal period, what struck me was the complex process a woman's body goes through.[26] What I learned is that researchers know that reproductive hormones indubitably play an integral role in postpartum affective dysregulation. However, there's no straight line we can trace to connect cause and effect. Postpartum disorder can be influenced by numerous other variables such as childhood or birth trauma, thyroid dysfunction, stress, sleep deprivation, personality pathologies, and other clinical diagnoses. So much more research is needed before we will be able to truly understand what triggers PPD – and how we can prevent or treat it.

As I immersed myself in the reproductive hormone literature, I was struck by how many *different* systems of the body are impacted during the perinatal period. Although by no means

26   Buckwalter, J. G., Stanczyk, F. Z., McCleary, C. A., Bluestein, B. W., Buckwalter, D. K., Rankin, K. P., Chang, L., & Goodwin, T. M. (1999). Pregnancy, the postpartum, and steroid hormones: effects on cognition and mood. *Psychoneuroendocrinology, 24*(1), 69–84. https://doi.org/10.1016/s0306-4530(98)00044-4

Glynn, L. M. (2010). Giving birth to a new brain: hormone exposures of pregnancy influence human memory. *Psychoneuroendocrinology, 35*(8), 1148–1155. https://doi.org/10.1016/j.psyneuen.2010.01.015

Perry, C. (2023, April 12). What to expect with postpartum hormone changes. *Parents.* https://www.parents.com/pregnancy/my-body/postpartum/postpartum-hormone-changes/

Schiller, C. E., Meltzer-Brody, S., & Rubinow, D. R. (2015). The role of reproductive hormones in postpartum depression. *CNS Spectrums, 20*(1), 48–59. https://doi.org/10.1017/S1092852914000480

xhaustive, I constructed a list of hormones involved in the perinatal period to provide a isualization. Does this evoke an appreciation for what your body just went through?

ake a moment to reflect on the complexities of hormonal fluctuation during the perinatal eriod. By acknowledging that you are undergoing yet another life transition as your body ttempts to physiologically stabilize (a process that can take significantly longer than the verage maternity leave), my hope is that with that you can offer yourself kindness. Should you xperience mood fluctuations, having this awareness can help you recognize that *one* possible mpetus could be attributable to hormone fluctuation.

Some of the Hormones involved in the Perinatal Period				
Steroidal hormones such as P, DHEA, and T	Lactogenic hormones such as Prolactin	Increased Cortisol and Adrenaline due to increased stressors	Sleep deprivation often impacts Melatonin, subsequently Serotonin	Estrogen and Progesterone

As your body works diligently to get back to normal after birth, remember that cortisol evels might be increased due to sleep deprivation. In turn, this can impact melatonin and subsequently serotonin. As if you needed more change, prolactin (the milk-making hormone), decreases with time and varies depending on length of breastfeeding. *So*, offer yourself some grace. If you find yourself weepy at work, perhaps your body is working hard to regulate those hormones. Wipe your tears and positively affirm how hard you are working and transitioning as an employed mama.

ANA H.

How to Pivot When Your Lactation Journey is Derailed

Ana Haver is an employed mother of two sons. She is a registered nurse, currently working in the role of a nursing care coordinator. Ana graduated from nursing school a few short months before delivering her first son. Ana is no stranger to hardship, nor to the necessity of pivoting when life throws you a curveball. At just five years old, Ana immigrated to the United States with her mother and siblings after her mother divorced her father who suffered from alcohol dependence. She acculturated in the best way she knew how, graduated from nursing school, and went on to marry the love of her life. A deeply personal decision, she was determined to exclusively nurse her son. Despite some initial struggles and consultation with a lactation consultant, she maintained a beautiful nursing journey with her son for thirteen months.

Thirteen months postpartum, she transitioned to a full-time nursing role as a labor and delivery nurse. The hospital was nearly an hour from her home, her shifts totaled 14–16 hours including the commute, and she had previously been working from home, allowing her to nurse on demand. Ana experienced debilitating separation anxiety. She was experiencing a parallel process as these two roles, mother and nurse, were both *new* and came with pressure to perform. Despite the support from her partner, her milk supply diminished. She experienced spoken and unspoken expectations from the hospital to perform as a newly registered nurse while operating in an understaffed, under-supported labor and delivery unit. This translated to frequent if/then statements. *If* I take a pumping break, *then* I will miss out on an opportunity to participate in the delivery of a baby, crucial to my learning experience. *If* I take a pumping break, *then* this could raise concern about my commitment to this role. "Becky, no one can prepare you to become a mom," she told me. "In your mind, you are thinking you will pump at work and will bring three to four bottles home. That did not happen. I underestimated how busy I would be." Many employed mothers can relate.

Ana's increased stress further diminished her supply and led to a premature weaning process, which was a source of grief. Ana reflected back on this experience, advising employed mothers to (1) *put your foot down and take your break to pump!* (2) adopt a positive mindset about pumping, (3) check internal and external expectations, and (4) be open and assertive with your supervisor about your intentions to pump. Another piece of advice Ana offers to employed mothers who do not want to or cannot double pump is to utilize *milkies*, a lactation gadget designed to catch milk from the alternative breast while nursing. These allowed her to save multiple bottles per week. She also recommends physically and mentally relaxing while pumping, hydrating, and nourishing your body with nutritious foods.

Fast forward to her second postpartum experience. A deeply personal decision, she desired to also nurse her second son. When he was seven months old, she transitioned into what is now her current role as a nursing care coordinator. During her training for this role, she developed biliary dyskinesia, requiring an emergency cholecystectomy. During her medical clearance for the cholecystectomy, her blood work revealed Hashimoto's Thyroiditis. Not without surprise, the surgery, in combination with an autoimmune diagnosis, impacted her milk supply. Can you imagine what a rollercoaster that week felt like for Ana? And how many mothers have

xperienced a similar rollercoaster during their lactation journey as they entered employed
motherhood? Although guilt crept in on occasion, Ana adopted a gratitude practice, focusing
on her health and ability to care for her boys, distinct from the amount of milk produced in
each duct. Ana continues to integrate gratitude practice in her daily life, which she recommends
to all employed mothers. "I still had my children. They were healthy regardless of my milk. I
earned this the hard way."

Dimension of Wellness:
Environmental

NOTES

_____

_____

_____

_____

_____

_____

_____

_____

_____

_____

_____

_____

_____

_____

_____

_____

_____

CHAPTER 5

ENVIRONMENTAL WELLNESS

Be Mindful of Your Environments

Your world has changed. It's the understatement of the century, and it still needs to be said. But not just that: as new working moms, we move in and out of so many different environments on such abbreviated time frames. (How's that for a neutral synonym for rush, hectic, chaotic…?)

After a short hospital stay for the delivery, you're back home – a home which probably looks pretty different with all the packages, deliveries, gifts, new furniture… Two days later, you're packing your first diaper to head to the pediatrician, which may be a totally unfamiliar space – and quite different from the OB/GYN where you had been spending so much of your time. When it's time to go back to work, your workplace probably looks a bit different too; you might have pumping gear to store, photos of your new family, and more healthy snacks in the desk drawer to keep you going.

Now you're starting to visit new social and commercial spaces, playgrounds and baby stores. You've got antennae raised around new issues: different parts of the political environment are impacting you directly, different laws and policies that you've never considered instantly become urgently relevant. You may even look at the natural environment around you with different eyes: How will deforestation, water pollution, and rising sea temperatures impact the new life you're holding in your arms?

It's hard not to experience whiplash. There will be times when you feel like everything is a blur, and you don't know which end is up. That's normal. The following chapter is meant to help you think through the ways you can be mindful of your environments and the transition between them, so that you can save as much of your energy as possible for the things that truly matter to you.

CREATE A FUNCTIONAL AND ORGANIZED HOME ENVIRONMENT – WITHOUT ADDING GUILT!

It seems like she's been around forever, but tidying guru Marie Kondo only took the English-speaking world by storm in 2014, with her book The Life-Changing Magic of Tidying Up: The Japanese Art of Decluttering and Organizing. While the principles are beautiful, inviting, and infinitely Instagrammable, I couldn't help but read her words about the effortless 'magic' of simply deciding which possessions no longer sparked 'joy' and moving them out the door. Reading her advice about prioritizing space over a stocked supply cabinet, it was hard to think of anything except: "This person doesn't have children." (And I know I wasn't alone.)

Flash forward to the present, and now the tidying guru has three young kids. Her house is more chaotic and, she realizes, she's okay with it. Her priorities have shifted.

Lots of people have used this shift to critique Kondo, but I say, if the household name in tidying is okay with giving herself grace now that she's a working mom, let's follow her lead.

in the advice that follows, I encourage you to take what works, leave what doesn't, and reach out to your fellow working moms for advice. When possible, hire someone to help, lower your expectations, simplify your processes, and be kind to yourself.

Home

Time is your one finite resource. Interacting with a disorganized or chaotic home environment costs you time. Time you could be spending playing with your little one, connecting with your partner, or filling your own cup. Today, home organizers are available for on-going work or one-time projects; consider investing in one to take something off your plate.

Early on, I learned early on the cost of a disorganized, chaotic environment. After leaving my pump at home multiple days in a row, I finally paused and ordered a bag hook to place next to the garage door. This required less than ten minutes from start to finish but saved me multiple trips back home and likely several hours of time, not to mention stress.

Here is an exercise to try (or delegate to your partner):

1. Walk into each room of your home and identify any changes to the environment that could increase everyday functioning.

2. Create a list of those changes, per room.

3. Tackle one room each weekend.

Tracking inventory can save you time and a tension headache. The last thing I wanted to spend my weekends doing was making multiple trips to the store. My partner and I found a smartphone app for tracking inventory. When our budget allowed, we eventually upgraded to a project management tool and created a separate item group for inventory. Divide and conquer was the name of the game. When one of us noticed a low stock item (toilet paper, diapers), we added it to the app, and the other person received a notification. Similarly, we collaboratively utilized a grocery shopping app. Several shopping apps offer a subscription option, which we utilized for pantry and baby care items.

Keeping a clean house is a losing battle. This was a hard one for me. I like my house clean. Not tidy, *clean*. After several weeks of putting myself into a tizzy, my partner and I constructed a daily cleaning schedule that felt much more manageable. (I include a sample list of a daily cleaning schedule below.) I also accepted that my house would not be *clean* for another few years. Yes, maybe I could relish a few clean minutes following a house cleaning service, but I had to come to terms with the fact that those minutes would be fleeting. I reduced cleanliness expectations, then reduced them again. Expecting a clean house only worsened the postpartum anxiety that was already paralyzing me.

I include a sample list of a daily cleaning schedule below. We also created a goal to pay off some debt in order to create space in budget for a house cleaning service. After a lot of discipline, we reached our goal and oh how it paid off. Worth. Every. Penny. We started at a monthly service but eventually moved to weekly after having our second.

We approached cleaning with a *divide and conquer* mindset. It sounds like a lot, but between the two of us, we never spent more than thirty minutes per day. I would also emphasize adopting a *good enough* approach. Someday your house will sparkle (if you want it to), but today is not that day, and that is okay.

CLEANING *checklist*

Everyday

- ☐ Meal/kitchen clean-up
- ☐ 1 load of laundry
- ☐ Put clothes away
- ☐ Wash bottles and pump parts
- ☐ Prep bag/items for tomorrow
- ☐ Sweep high traffic areas

Monday
{ KITCHEN }

- ☐ Clean out fridge
- ☐ Wipe microwave
- ☐ Sweep/vacuum
- ☐ Clean sink
- ☐ Wipe cabinets
- ☐ Stovetop

Tuesday
{ BATHROOMS }

- ☐ Disinfect counters and sinks
- ☐ Mop floor
- ☐ Clean shower/tub
- ☐ Clean toilets
- ☐ Replace towels
- ☐ Clean bath toys

Wednesday
{ LIVING ROOM }

- ☐ Pick up and organize toys
- ☐ Wash or disinfect toys, if needed
- ☐ Vacuum *prior to vacuuming, check floor for chokeable items*

Thursday
{DINING RM OR OFFICE }

- ☐ Clean floors
- ☐ Declutter / Organize
- ☐ Dust furniture

Friday
{ BEDROOMS }

- ☐ Vacuum
- ☐ Wash and change sheets (including pillowcases and crib sheets)
- ☐ Pick up / Organize

Weekend
{ OTHER }

- ☐ Garage
- ☐ Clean car
- ☐ Outdoor / yard
- ☐ Windows, blinds
- ☐ Holiday prep
- ☐ Closets / pantry

Buy. Less. Stuff. Despite marketing efforts intended to convince you that you *need* every baby toy or gadget under the sun, babies do not need much. Babies. Do. Not. Need. Much. In fact, the more *stuff* you have, the more *stuff* you will have to manage. After spending a precious weekend organizing and sorting through buckets and buckets of baby stuff, I decided to adopt a minimalist mindset. Management of *stuff* was (1) taking away time from my precious daughters, (2) exhausting and cyclical, and (3) not bringing me any joy.

I use the term *minimalist* loosely as I know better than to use motherhood and minimalism in the same sentence. A minimalist mindset, though, can help guide your household management decisions. It will ultimately allow you to spend more time with those you love.

Questions I routinely asked myself when decluttering:

- Have I used this item in the last 30 days?

- Is there a high likelihood that I will use this item in the next 30-60 days? If not, can I pass it on to an expectant mother or donate it?

- Do I already have this item or a similar item?

- Is this item *actually* useful?

- Is this item positively contributing to the functionality of everyday life?

It's easier than ever to rehome objects we don't need, without that twinge of guilt that we're dumping things into a landfill. Local "Buy Nothing" groups on social media allow you to connect with neighbors who need what you have. It can be a great way to build community, too.

Environmental cues for activity transitions. Remember the graceful dance of mindful multitasking? Your environment can help you transition between activities by providing cues that let your five senses know it's time to switch gears. One mother I interviewed intentionally created *Friday Night* cues to help her body slow down after a long week managing both work and motherhood responsibilities. Putting on her slippers, getting out the same green, warm, comfy blanket, and popping popcorn provided a full sensory experience through sounds, textures, visuals, and smells to induce relaxation.

Environmental change to reset and recharge. If you're struggling because you feel glued to your chair, try walking outside for some fresh air or remove any stress inducers from your office. If you're struggling because you're stuck in your pjs, try going to an environment you know will stimulate your mind and rejuvenate your energy levels. Alternatively, avoid environments that cause undue stress. I found intentional environmental changes especially necessary in the winter months when days are short, cold, and dreary. At times, all it took was a quick visit to an indoor mall or a drive to the local coffee shop to feel like myself again. Most importantly, pay attention to *when* you need an environmental change so you can be proactive.

The vicious cycle of maintaining a clean (and functional) car. When you're in multitasking mode, it can be easy to let your car turn into a catchall space. Part office, part toy museum, part…garbage dump? Your car should be a means of transportation, ideally not one that makes you feel like the walls are closing in on you, with all the empty applesauce pouches and baby toys filling it to the brim.

Below are some tips on car maintenance for employed motherhood.

- Empty trash every time you get gas, enter daycare, or go to the carwash.

- Invest in a car wash subscription. I found that this paid for itself after two to three car washes. It can also be a productive use of time should your little one fall asleep in the car.

- Create a habit of bringing everything in from the car upon arrival home (older siblings can help with this!).

- Purchase a car organizer for toys, baby items, and wipes. You will need them.

- Create a diaper changing station in the trunk of your car for emergency or regular use.

- Keep a towel in your car at all times for mishaps and emergencies.

take Care of your environments and your environments will take of YOU!

CREATE A HEALTHY WORKSPACE

There is no better time to evaluate the functionality of your workspace than when coming back to the office after several weeks away. Take inventory, assess functionality, and make the time to rearrange and organize. If you will be pumping in your office, for example, make necessary changes to set up a pumping area. On your first day back, block out at least an hour to focus on your workspace. Consider the return on investment: an hour of rearranging and organization can save countless hours. Save yourself the time and energy. Refer to Chapter 4, *Pumping in the Workplace* section for tips on making your office conducive to lactation.

For moms who are returning to work within the home, do this assessment far enough in advance of your first day for you to take steps to improve it. Ask yourself what you see when you're at your desk. If you're looking out a window, what might you be able to improve with your view? Can you add a birdfeeder? If you don't have a window, think about what image you want to look at when you're at your desk – something relaxing? Energizing? While all homes have constraints, take advantage of the fact that you are your own office manager. Make the office work for you!

Other things to think about:

- How is your lighting? Can you add a desk lamp or floor lamp to brighten up the space? (Try your lighting on a video call and adjust as needed: either buy a dedicated light or play with the settings on your camera/monitor)

- Do you want music or noise-canceling headphones to get you in the zone and avoid distractions?

- If your child will be cared for in the home, do you have a place to store snacks and breast milk (if pumping), so that you can grab a bite to eat without disrupting your caregiver?

- Do you have a plan for how to handle interruptions by kids or pets? (Points for creativity!!)

CONNECT WITH YOUR NEIGHBORHOOD AND COMMUNITY

No matter your level of connection with your neighborhood and community, your experience as an employed mother will change the way you relate to your surroundings. For me, it opened my eyes to a world of resources and opportunities as well as some frustrations. I found parks, library programs, community centers, and city events I never knew existed but also encountered some under-resourced aspects of our community such as missing diaper changers in *most* restaurants. By leaning into your community during your transition back to employment, you can increase your sense of community and decrease binary thinking of *employed* versus *stay-at-home* mom. When you feel comfortable co-existing in all of these various environments, it will feel positive and productive.

Parks

Once I opened a county parks and recreation map, I developed a greater appreciation for the amount and variety of parks throughout my county. As my partner and I explored a few different parks, we found a few within walking distance, and a few we preferred to drive to. The one closest to our home presented some safety concerns – goodbye 1950's seesaw! We contacted our country parks and recreation director to inform her of our concerns. We received a response within a business day and were included in the playground redesign. As we spread the word and consulted with a few other neighbors, this created a collective team effort amongst parents in our neighborhood, centering around the collective purpose of developing a safe and fun place for our children to play. I met numerous mothers – employed *and* stay-at-home – which ultimately increased our quantity and quality of neighborhood and community interactions. And bonus, it increased our physical activity.

Library Programs

Your library system is another way to connect with your community. You also cannot beat *free*! We primarily attended Saturday and Sunday programming, which connected me with other employed mothers who also could not attend during the week. By participating in recurring programs, familiar faces became acquaintances who gradually evolved to family friends. Weekend programming also allows your children to maintain a daily routine; if we made a concerted effort to schedule a morning activity, naptime was less of a struggle. We also found the daycare transition on Monday morning to be smoother if we had maintained a semblance of a routine on the weekend.

Community Centers

Community centers are another resource that can provide enriching activities on the weekends or on holidays when you are off work. Community holiday events are often hosted at community centers and can be an opportunity to meet other employed mothers. I have also found that recreational and playgroups occur either weekly or monthly, so perhaps sign up for their weekly email or newsletter to stay up to date on events. Some of my fondest memories involve attending a "baby and me" yoga class at one of our community centers. Not only was it a great workout and bonding experience with my baby, but it also was a gentle reminder of just how many postpartum moms (many of them likely employed) were in my community.

INTERACTING WITH YOUR BROADER ENVIRONMENTS

Accessing Support and Resources

Employed motherhood is part of the world's evolutionary processes. Organizations with missions focused on supporting employed mothers are predominantly in their infancy. Nonetheless, there *is* an abundance of resources. The world is your oyster. It might require a tedious Dr. Google search or two, but you will find what you need.

The organization *Moms Rising* not only provides information for mothers, but also hosts campaigns on topics to support employed mothers (e.g., workplace and maternal justice) and online community platforms. The *National Partnership for Women & Families* supports employed mothers through its mission to "improve the lives of women and families by achieving equality for all women." You can also conduct a state-wide search for organizations within your state.

Activism

Taking action is another way to positively impact the climate for employed mothers. Do what you can in this season or rest assured that you can take a more active role at state, national, or international levels at a later time. If taking action *now* is the therapy you need, there are numerous ways to do so. Some examples include (1) participate in or organize a protest or march, (2) *vote* for candidates that advocate policy reform to help working mothers, (3) call or write to your elected officials, or (4) write to various media sources. In a moment of frustration, I called my Governor's Office to advocate for paid parental leave. Although it fell on deaf ears, I felt empowered versus victimized knowing I was taking action versus internalizing my frustration.

Paying It Forward

In time, perhaps years after reading this, pay it forward when an opportunity presents itself. I know I could have benefited from this book when I was returning to work, so nearly three years after my transition back following my second parental leave, I mustered the brain power and energy to write it. My way of paying it forward. Specific ways to pay it forward might include:

(1) donating to a meaningful cause

(2) volunteering (many employers now offer 16 hours of annual volunteer leave)

(3) mentoring other newly employed mothers (formally or informally) (4) writing and publishing about your transition to employed motherhood.

Take Care of Mother Earth

Our feet are grounded to the earth, to Mother Earth, by gravity. Each day, each moment, is a gift to spend another day on Mother Earth. Honor this gift by making small, simple changes to care for her as you simultaneously care gently for yourself. I remember searching for office paces as I established my private practice. After commuting for the past decade in my car, on buses, on the Metro, I was determined to no longer *live that life*. I focused on finding a space close to home, accessible on the local bus route and close enough to bicycle to.

After a few weeks in my new office, I started to pay attention to the time I was saving, the gasoline I was not buying, and the beauty of my short commute. There was one particular cherry blossom tree that seemed to bloom before all the others and pushed its blossom well beyond others. I learned to appreciate the sound of rain as it hit the sidewalk and I leaned into all of the sounds when I needed a mindful moment. Was *I* helping Mother Earth or was she helping *me*? In short, consider ways to embrace a greener commute.

Some additional ways to care for Mother Earth:

- Invest in a reusable coffee mug or tumbler, water bottle, straws and utensils. These products are not all created equal, so give yourself permission to shop around.

- Try reusable breast pads, eco-friendly diapers and wipes.

- Recycle / compost whenever possible. (Many towns offer free composting services, while others have subscription-based options. Community gardens also may take food scraps.)

- Reduce consumption, for example by using thrift stores, or your local "Buy Nothing" group.

- Invest in a professional capsule wardrobe.

- Utilize public transportation, if possible.

- Reuse shopping bags.

- Spend time in nature – with your baby, alone, on your lunch break, for exercise, with your friends or partner. Any activity you can do outside, try it. As I learned on my commute, the relationship with the outdoors goes both ways.

Employed moms change the world!

Dimension of Wellness:
Financial

NOTES

CHAPTER 6

FINANCIAL WELLNESS

Because, well, children are expensive.

"How much does it cost per month to have a child?" My ears perked up as I overheard a newly married couple earnestly ask this question to a new mom during a backyard barbecue. I waited for her reply, but none came, just the sounds of nervous, incredulous laughter. When the laughter subsided, I heard the new mom say, "A lot. I don't know. You don't want to know."

All families relate to their finances in their own way, but there's nothing like the whirlwind of a new baby to add a dose of uncertainty to even the most organized financial plan. Today, we're seeing new wild swings in the economy, as the pandemic has shifted people's child care decisions and – often – increased the costs. Waitlists at daycares, bidding wars over nannies – it's a lot!

When new factors like the cost of childcare – which can vary widely depending on the kind and amount of care you need, as well as your geographic location – get mixed into family life that has already been transformed physically and emotionally, it can be particularly challenging to stay the course. Numerous clients have vented to me about how they impulsively submitted a resignation once they calculated the paltry *take home* pay that would have been left once their decent salary got devoured by childcare and other new expenses. I also heard those same mothers regret having made such a decision without carefully considering the *bigger picture,* once they recognized in hindsight that they had constructed their formula in a state of exhaustion and stress. Other mothers who remained in the workforce expressed gratitude for that decision but regretted not having taken full advantage of various fiscal or tax benefits offered by their employer.

When you are up to your neck in change, it is easy to overlook all of the ways working motherhood can influence your personal finances. Be kind to yourself: you *can* maintain and nourish your financial health during this life transition. Let's start with a simple exercise to identify (1) short-term financial benefits to remaining in the workforce and (2) long-term financial benefits to remaining in the workforce. What are three short-term financial benefits to remaining in the workforce? What are three long-term financial benefits to remaining in the workforce? (Refer to Appendix F for the written exercise.)

MAINTAIN PERSPECTIVE

When you cannot see the forest through the trees, it is easy to lose sight of a simple truth: the financial strain of diapers, childcare, and sanity-preserving impulse purchases will come to an end. It *will* pass. You will not pay a mortgage-equivalent childcare bill forever. I *promise.*

This is also a season to gently consider your sanity. Don't be *penny wise, pound foolish.* If you need to spend $5-10 extra per week for grocery delivery, spend the money. Spend. The. Money. If you are sacrificing your mental health to save a few bucks here and there, give yourself permission to outsource or pay for professional support. For example, if you are spending multiple nights exhausted and tearful on the nursery floor, hire a sleep consultant. Feel all of your feelings, then pivot where you need to pivot. If it means spending some money, spend it. There will be a return on your investment.

Don't be Penny wise, Pound foolish!

CONTROLLING IMPULSES WHEN CRISIS MODE HITS

There will be a time when crisis mode takes over. Whether it be your child's first cold or buying every bottle under the sun because your infant refuses a bottle a week before returning to work, it will come. For me, it happened after the full week of daycare. My daughter spiked a high fever and – conveniently – our thermometer broke. At 11 p.m., I drove to the one open store near us, which did not have any pediatric thermometers in stock. I finally found two decent (enough) thermometers at a pharmacy that cost a small fortune. Then, after returning home and realizing how terrible the reviews were online, I ended up purchasing two more online. You get the picture. To make a long story short, we ended up in the ER, realizing that neither of our thermometers were reliable. Regardless, everyone lived to tell the story. What I wish I had done is take a deep breath and slow down. Yes, fevers are scary, but crisis mode turned into a frenetic, impulsive search for the perfect thermometer.

Clients often tell another common story, about that one *terrible, sleepless* night during which you purchase every sleep training book in existence. Recognize that you've had one bad night; that does not make your baby a bad sleeper. Take a deep breath, try to rest, and regroup in the morning to prevent impulsive spending. You'll likely spend a small fortune on something you truly do not need.

ASKING FOR A RAISE AND/OR BONUS

No doubt, you are returning to work with a new set of skills, transferrable to the workplace. Your skills are valuable and *can* translate to increased pay or financial incentive. This is the time to stand confident in your abilities. If negative self-talk occurs, reframe.

Here are two examples:

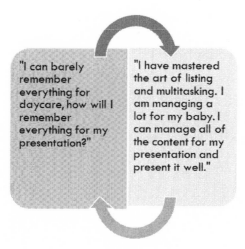

"I can barely remember everything for daycare, how will I remember everything for my presentation?"

"I have mastered the art of listing and multitasking. I am managing a lot for my baby. I can manage all of the content for my presentation and present it well."

Practice highlighting the skills you have worked hard to develop that *can* translate to financial compensation. Or envision yourself in upper management. What attributes would you want in a boss? Here are some examples of how motherhood translates to the workplace.

- Clear boundaries & priorities

- Management of high stress situations

- Mindful pairing

- Increased empathy

- Time management

- Commitment

- Quick & creative problem solving

Here is what worked for me.

1. Request a meeting with your direct supervisor to discuss a pay increase.

2. Prior to the meeting, prepare concrete, tangible examples of high performance and merit. Avoid tangents outside of performance scope (e.g., personal hardship, childcare, etc.). Be prepared to provide a specific number. I requested a 20% increase and was provided 18%. I was hoping for at least 10% so I was pleased with the outcome. My advice is to increase your minimal expectation by 5%.

3. Remain positive. Keep breathing. Highlight your strengths. Repeat.

4. If the meeting occurred without meeting notes or informally, write a memo and send a copy to your supervisor.

5. If you are provided an *immediate declination*, submit a written request to revisit the conversation in a specified timeframe (3/6/9 months).

6. Remember, the worst your employer can say is no, and even a hard *no* can be revisited at a later time.

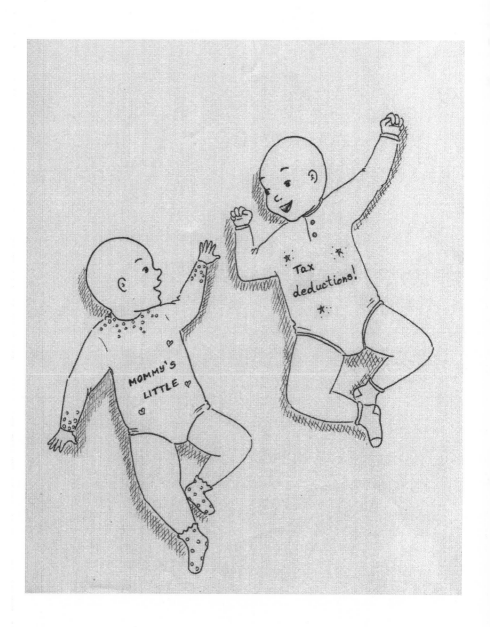

After my second parental leave, I was also practicing privately. This presented a new set of challenges: how do I honor myself in the form of a pay raise? I blocked out some time and crunched some numbers. My ultimate goal was to reduce my hours by five hours per week without losing revenue. I increased my hourly rate accordingly and contacted the two insurance companies with which I worked to request an evaluation of my reimbursement rates. Within two weeks, both insurance companies offered revised contracts, both increasing my hourly rates by over 15%. It was a good reminder that life transitions can create a healthy, productive pause. Had there not been an impetus for contacting these insurance companies, how long would I have been complacent with my current rates?

Here are some considerations if self-employed:

- Perform a market comparison. If you are undercharging, adjust accordingly.

- Start backwards when number crunching. What is your desired salary? Start with that number, then divide accordingly.

- Reduce overhead, if possible.

- Strategize and maximize tax incentives. I increased my Self-Employment Plan IRA monthly contribution, which reduced my tax rate. I also improved my bookkeeping, which prevented loss of potential write-offs.

FINANCIAL FITNESS

Prior to having children, I naively anticipated a few added expenses, but never in my wildest dreams could I have imagined spending the amount of money I did, especially in the newborn and infant phase. Diapers are *not* cheap, not to mention childcare akin to a mortgage. After a humbling financial transition to parenthood, and prior to conceiving our second child, my partner and I nourished our financial wellness. We ate a full portion of crow pie, utilized his Employee Assistance Benefit, and consulted with a financial advisor. This was not any type of *magic wand* approach, but it provided us with some tangible, concrete ways to improve our financial health and pave the way to make it even possible to maintain our financial health with a second child.

Emotional and Financial Wellness Go Hand-in-Hand

There are a lot of spreadsheets and calculations that go into establishing financial wellness, but don't forget to take into account the intangible influences that might well have an impact. When I neglected my emotional health, I noticed increased impulse purchases – specifically items to compensate for separation anxiety – and disregard for our budget during periods of high stress. If this resonates with you, take this as a gentle reminder of the importance of nourishing all areas of wellness, as there is a bidirectional relationship between them all.

Here are some tangible, concrete ways to maintain your financial health during this season of life.[27] Remember, from an HR perspective, having a child qualifies as a *life event*, which should allow you to modify your employment benefits upon your return to work.

Budgeting

Transition periods can create a natural pause. By this point, you likely have a better idea of the *new normal* in terms of additional budget items to integrate. My partner and I identified new expenses by brainstorming with the help of a good old fashioned paper and pen. Once we identified new budget items and accompanying costs, we updated our master budget on Excel.

Some useful finance and budgeting tools include:

- Mint
- EveryDollar
- Spendee
- Mobills
- YNAB
- Honeydue (for couples)

As you update your family budget, you might want to include (1) childcare, (2) babysitters as needed, (3) diapering, (4) clothing (budget for *both* mom and baby), (5) formula, (6) lactation supplies (breast pads, nursing bras, pump replacement parts, etc.), (7) medical bills and increased premiums, (8) baby equipment, and (9) family vacations. Automating any of these expenses can save you time and mental energy, allowing you to outsource some of the many balls you're trying to keep in the air.

MAKE FINANCES A HABIT

When life gets hectic, it can be easy to fly on autopilot. No judgment – it's just logical that we put our attention toward the things (ahem, people) that are screaming for it, and let everything else slide a little bit. But the saying, "knowledge is power," holds true for finances, whether you're an employee or self-employed, whether you keep the family books or let your partner take the lead.

If you tend to let your partner handle the family finances, now isn't the time to try a DIY MBA; but it is time to ask for overall updates about the state of your family budget. Stick to the basics: How's the monthly cash flow? How are retirement savings? What do other savings goals look like?

---

27   Ellis, K. (2023, Spring 17). 10 best ways to save for college. *Ramsey.* https://www.ramseysolutions.com/saving/saving-for-college-is-easier-than-you-think

f you're the family accountant, try to do the same for your partner, to make sure they are ooped into what's going on and help out as necessary. That's the only way to make sure veryone is on the same page with expenses. When both people have a clear sense of the udget, impulsive decisions become harder to make, and it becomes easier to make important nvestments – say hiring an occasional night-nurse to help with sleep – when both people can ee how it impacts the bottomline.

Regardless of who plays which role, to get on the same page with your partner, you've got to nake the time. In order to intentionally nourish some of these dimensions of wellness, my partner and I committed to forming a habit of checking in with each other weekly, monthly, and annually. Super sexy, right? Very sexy, actually, if by the end of the year you have maintained inancial health and can enjoy a family vacation or trip to the spa! For us, we strived to maintain ach area of wellness because our goal was to live to work, not work to live. Our check-ins nelped us stay the course in that we were able to spend more quality time with those we loved nost.

Jse these check-ins as a chance to gauge where you are now, whether your postpartum experience has ramped up your desire to work, curbed your motivation – or left you roughly in he same head and heart space you were in previously. Your partner, if you have one, may also ve experiencing changes in terms of finances and goals, in the postpartum period; they may vant to scale back work to spend more quality time with the family, or feel a need to intensify heir commitment in order to grow the family nest egg. Make room to explore and honor hese feelings as they relate to the family budget.

Weekly

Setting up weekly financial check-ins – with your partner if you have one – can serve as both an evaluative tool and reset for the following week. If you're parenting solo, consider finding an accountability partner, like another solo parent, a supportive relative, or a financially savvy friend. (You don't have to disclose personal information if that doesn't feel right; just use this person to check in, discuss your goals, successes and struggles.)

Here is what worked for my partner and me.

1. Establish a day and a time. We chose Friday night as it helped us stay on track during the weekend. It also worked for us in that we wanted to focus on rest and quality family time during the weekend. The last way we wanted to spend our precious weekend was talking about money. You might feel differently. Figure out a system that works for you and your family.

2. Identify what you *do* and *don't* want to focus on. We kept these check-ins informal and low pressure. As long as there were no major aberrations from the budget, we moved on with our night.

3. When we found any consistent aberrations from the budget, we agreed to compassionately discuss and identify solutions.

Monthly and Quarterly

The monthly and quarterly financial check-ins provided another pause to take our financial temperature. My youngest is now nearing three and the habit we created several years ago remains foundational to our financial health.

For monthly financial check-ins, here is what worked for my partner and me.

1. Designate the same time period each month. For us, it was the last Friday of every month. We tried to make these conversations enjoyable and judgment free. We enjoyed a cocktail or glass of wine together, which made the experience less sucky. Remember, this is a busy, exhausting season of life. Be kind and offer compassion.

2. Identify any aberrations from the budget and brainstorm solutions.

3. Designate a physical space in your home to store *one-time* bills due by the end of the month. We chose a kitchen drawer. Automate anything that can be.

4. Pay bills from the designated *monthly* drawer. We used the *divide and conquer* approach.

5. Identify any upcoming expenses.

Some of the common monthly check-in activities for us included submitting receipts to our Dependent Care Flexible Spending Account (DCFSA), paying one-time bills, and coordinating birthday gifts for family members. We utilized a similar approach for quarterly financial check-ins, which we designated as the last Friday of the month of each quarter. For example, quarter one was the last Friday of March. Some of the common topics of quarterly check-ins included nanny taxes, gifts for childcare providers (this was important to intentionally thank childcare at least once per quarter), and car insurance, which was quarterly. I used this time to evaluate my private practice revenue, pay quarterly taxes, and reflect on my personal financial goals such as my SEP retirement contributions, revenue goals, and overall financial health. Sometimes this was as simple as logging into my accounts and reviewing my statements, listening to an entrepreneur podcast focused on financial sustainability, or brainstorming ways to reduce my overhead costs. You do not have to have a Ph.D. in finance to nourish your financial fitness. Brief yet focused check-ins can yield results.

Annually

My partner and I launch our annual financial check-in around the time that our companies present the upcoming employee benefits. Once we marinate in the changes and crunch numbers, we book a sitter and plan for at least two hours of time together focused on our annual financial health of the current and upcoming year. We also present individual financial goals in support of one another.

Taxes. Since I also run a private practice and am self-employed, I evaluate and predict – using metrics from previous years – how I am doing saving for taxes and maximizing tax deductions. This is not something I integrate into our annual check-in, but it is typically an impetus and eminder to pause and assess my upcoming tax responsibilities. I save at least 30% of all evenue for tax contributions.

Selecting employee benefits. We incorporate benefit selections into our annual financial heck-in. This often includes *making a case* for why we individually believe a particular selection hould or should not be made. Last year we went back-and-forth about whether or not to nclude long-term disability and additional life insurance.

Emergency budget. Financial emergencies happen. I cannot recall a single year that we did not have at least two major financial emergencies. One particular year our furnace needed eplacement totaling over $8k, and then one month later our daughter needed a tonsillectomy, which, even after medical benefits, cost over $1,500. This was a hard year financially and used every penny of our emergency budget.

Individual goals. I benefit from sharing my individual financial goals with my partner. In part, I enjoy his verbal support. In part, when I say my goals out loud, I feel more accountable to myself. Your hard work and discipline are worth celebrating. Neurologically, the more you pause to celebrate all of your benchmarks, the more dopamine and serotonin you release. As you create this positive feedback loop, you gain momentum, and what once seemed like an uphill climb becomes second nature.

Donations. Individually and collaboratively, we identify meaningful non-profit organizations for annual donations. This is an important aspect of our annual financial check-in and allows us to lean into others. Personally, I know that if I increase my revenue, I can positively contribute to a meaningful cause, which ultimately increases my motivation to stay the course.

OTHER FINANCIAL RECOMMENDATIONS

Create a will.

This is as much about designating a caretaker in the case of your death as much as it is outlining financial distribution. Sometimes Employee Assistance Programs (EAP) offer legal assistance as a free benefit which can include wills and trusts.

Automate bills.

If possible, automate as many bills as possible. This will be one less task taken off your plate. If the bill cannot be automated, divide the responsibility with your partner.

Swap or trade with other parents.

If you feel comfortable, swap babysitting or baby items with friends and family.

In-home childcare for multiples & siblings close in age.

Consider in-home childcare for multiples or siblings close in age. Often times, it can be less expensive [and more convenient!] for in-home care when factoring in more than one child.

Childcare Payroll.

If you hire a nanny, there are numerous nanny payroll services which can save you time managing payroll and taxes.

COMMON BENEFITS
OFFERED BY EMPLOYERS

Employee Assistance Program (EAP)

EAP often provides free counseling, financial consultation, and legal services.

Childcare

Either onsite or emergency coordination of childcare.

Medical Benefits

Having a baby qualifies as a life event which should allow you to modify your benefits upon your return to work.

Retirement Matching

Some companies offer as much as six percent matching of any contributions.

Flexible Spending Account

An FSA allows you pay for out-of-pocket medical expenses with tax-free dollars. Approved expenses include insurance copayments and deductibles, qualified prescription drugs, and medical devices.

Typically following our monthly financial check-ins, I'd say something like, "Oh my God, I am spending a small fortune on childcare! I have to quit! Tomorrow!" I was grateful (and proud) of my salary, but truthfully, there was not much left over when all the things were paid for. I was not sitting in a corner office making the annual bonus to pay for my nanny. The point? Your employee benefits provide additional streams of income that can ease the financial burden of working motherhood. When crunching numbers, integrate these benefits, in addition to all of the upward mobility and potential for pay increases that come from remaining in the workforce.

Dimension of Wellness:
Occupational

Gently Ease Back into the Workplace

NOTES

CHAPTER 7

OCCUPATIONAL WELLNESS

Thriving in the Workplace as a Mother

WHAT I LEARNED FROM STUDYING PARENTAL LEAVES

irst and foremost, there is a paucity of research on employed mothers in the workforce, let alone transitioning back to work from maternity leave. (Are you detecting a pattern here?) Secondly, due to large discrepancies in leave provided from country to country, it is difficult to generalize one body of research conducted in one country to another. For example, there was no way of extrapolating some of the findings from European, Canadian, and Scandinavian countries to the United States. Many of the studies were inconclusive. When I tried to find follow-up studies, I learned none existed. I hired a research assistant to ensure that I had not missed something from my literature review. My research assistant came up with similar results.

What we *did* discover through our research:[28]

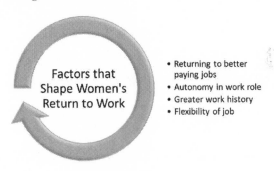

Factors that Shape Women's Return to Work

- Returning to better paying jobs
- Autonomy in work role
- Greater work history
- Flexibility of job

YOUR TRANSITION BACK. HOLD ON TIGHT.

Out of the frying pan and into the fire is not an adage you need to endorse in this life transition. Offer yourself an abundance of compassion and gentleness as you make your transition. Gently easing back into the workplace can support a healthy transition.

One approach to your transition back to work is a 2-3-4-5 model.

Week 1: Return to work for a 2-day work week

Week 2: Increase to a 3-day work week

Week 3: Increase to a 4-day work week

Week 4: Transition to a full 5-day work week.

28   Clark, C., & Gallagher, S. K. (2017). The influence of state maternity leave policies on US mothers' employment. *Community, Work & Family, 20*(4), 459–478. https://doi.org/10.1080/13668803.2016.1227769

Other options include: a hybrid remote/in-person schedule – whether you keep a set schedule (3 in-person/2 at home) or start primarily remote and work up to your in-person target; or a half-day model. Another idea is to return on a Friday with the goal to work remotely and sift through emails. You can also use this day as a trial childcare day. This can *get your feet wet* and familiarize you with all of the changes that happened while you were on leave. Reviewing all of these changes from home can give you the space to process, strategize responses without the pressure of colleagues present, and bonus, you have the weekend to prepare for an in-person return. Sorting through weeks or months of emails can be mentally and emotionally exhausting. Allow yourself the space to experience a wide spectrum of emotions from the comfort of your home.

If transitioning back to work *and* starting childcare during the same week feels like too much, have your partner take leave during the week of your return to cover childcare. This is a transition for everyone: yourself, your partner, your child, your employer, etc. Gently ease back. If you have the flexibility, consider selecting your return week with a built-in holiday. If lactating, remember to start building up a store of milk ahead of your return to avoid the feeling of pressure to produce a certain quantity during your first week. Begin pumping at least a month before your return and have your partner bottle feed. If your baby is anything like my second, it might take trying a few (or *ten!*) different bottles before you find one that your baby will take.

Thanks to the nature of my work and the closeness of my work team, I brought my daughter to the office one week before my return. This *exposed* me to the office, which I had not stepped foot in for several months, and reminded my colleagues of my nearing return. When I needed to nurse her during this visit, it was a gentle reminder that I needed to begin preparing my workspace for pumping. Following *your* first day – maybe on your commute back home, if you have the bandwidth – identify *what worked* and *work could have gone better*. This is a major life transition, so you should expect some things to go well and other things to need fine-tuning. Do not judge the day, just examine it. Brainstorm and write down in two separate columns *what went well* and *what could have gone better* (Appendix G). Find your rhythm. It's typical for stress to increase during any life transition, as your body goes on high alert in response to the myriad changes. With increased stress, the brain magnifies the negatives and distorts reality: this is a survival mechanism that is part of our evolutionary inheritance. Regular, positive self-talk and deep breathing can help quiet your survival instincts and remind yourself "I've got this."

When stress and angst led me down the rabbit hole, I was grateful to have the self-awareness to stop and check myself – especially when I got triggered by something totally unexpected: positive emotions and intellectual stimulation. I had focused *so* heavily on the "what if's" and "to-do's" that I had neglected the potential positives of returning to work. Some of the moments of triggering sounded like, "Here I am belly laughing and exchanging stories with Lara while my daughter is likely screaming from hunger and refusing yet another bottle." Catastrophizing? Yep. Did I catch myself? Yep. At that moment, I drew upon my own therapeutic toolbox and untangled those two thoughts: "I can enjoy belly laughing and adult conversation while also thinking about my daughter's wellbeing. I can also lean into the positive aspects of returning to work without labeling myself." If/ *then* statements can get you nto trouble. If you are belly laughing with a colleague or relishing a stimulating training, you are simply belly laughing and enjoying a training. It does *not* have to be accompanied by a *then* statement. "If I enjoy my work, *then* it must mean [fill in the blank]."

Another cognitive behavioral tool I utilized to respond to triggers is known as "S-T-O-P," which stands for Stop (pause, catch yourself, maintain self-awareness), Think (What's happening for me right now? What are my automatic thoughts?), Observe (What is my body telling me? Where do I feel the triggering in my body? What are my automatic emotions?), and Proceed (What is the best course? How can I reframe my thinking? Am I "should-ing" on myself?). I printed out a small stop sign and discreetly displayed it in my workspace as a gentle reminder to utilize S-T-O-P whenever triggered.

Celebrate. Taking a moment or the entire evening celebrating surviving your first day back will promote serotonin and dopamine, hormones to combat all of the adrenaline and cortisol released throughout your day. Open a bottle of champagne, take a bubble bath, order take-out, turn on some upbeat music, and dance in the living room. You did it. Your baby did it. Your partner did it. Go ahead and celebrate!

In the spirit of identifying *wins*, remember that your child will have positive experiences, not solely growing pains. When I reunited with my first daughter after my first day back at work, I will never forget Ms. Wendi. Her positive energy was palpable. She was wise. She was patient. She saw my daughter. *Really* saw my daughter. I knew upon my return that my daughter and Wendi had formed a special bond. This was a win for my daughter. *She* had formed a new bond with another adult who went on to teach her life lessons that she still draws upon today.

Reconnect. Reconnect with your little one and partner. Tell your baby all about your day. Savor some quality time together. This is an opportunity to begin establishing rituals for reconnection after a busy day and to practice mindfulness. This is also a time to exchange perspectives on *what went well* and *what could have gone better* with your partner. Identify ways to maintain *what went well* and potential solutions and strategies for *what could have gone better*. This is also a time to reconnect with your partner. How did each of you individually experience today? How can you validate and empathize with each other's experiences, especially if they are different? What does reconnection with your partner look like?

Decompress. This was a big day. Perhaps adrenaline permeates your system or, alternatively, you have beautifully detoxed to the point your eyelids feel like five-pound weights. What do you need to decompress? What is your body telling you? This *was* a monumental day, and it is okay to *not* be okay. It is okay to take some time to intentionally reflect, journal, meditate, take a slow walk, stretch your body, watch some television, or call a loved one. No matter the method, be gentle and self-compassionate after having undergone such a tremendous transition.

INAPPROPRIATE QUESTIONS AND UNSOLICITED COMMENTS

No matter how low you believe the odds are that someone in your office could ask an inappropriate question or make unsolicited comments that might evoke a visceral response or a – WTF?!? – scream inside your head, all I can say is, "Prepare." Not only can I personally attest to the horrific questions and statements that exit the mouths of some of the most accomplished and *well-mannered* colleagues, but speaking to hundreds of postpartum women as my profession, I hear – on the daily – some of these comments experienced by employed mothers who are in the depths of transitioning back to work after having a baby. Before I narrate some of these horror stories, allow me to qualify what I am about to outline. *Most* of the questions and comments are benign. Certainly, something to keep in mind before you swing a punch or notify HR. *But* explanations are not excuses for bad behavior. This is where you come in. How do *you* want to handle inappropriate questions or unsolicited comments? What will guide you in developing a decision tree for your responses?

As I mentioned earlier, following the birth of my second daughter I was employed part-time at an emergency psychiatric department. It was fast paced. There were police in-and-out with detained patients and, at times, family members crying in the room over, learning that their loved ones had experienced their first psychotic break or attempted suicide. Screaming and yelling were familiar sounds, as were periods of silence. The setup of the office space was akin to a fishbowl so if something happened, *everyone* was privy. The setup was well-intended with safety in mind. Should a floridly psychotic patient become highly agitated, we were there to step in and assist. As my pregnancy progressed, my colleagues witnessed it all. I was one lucky mom (SIKE!) to experience prodrome labor for over six weeks. Alas, when I would walk to the copy machine or to the kitchen, my painful contraction was witnessed by all. I share this to provide context. What are the unique factors in your workplace and how can this inform your responses to questions or unsolicited comments? For me, boundaries in my office were more diffuse than your typical workplace, and I kept this in mind when triaging interactions and my subsequent response.

When I brought my daughter to the office prior to my first day back, you can imagine the flock of colleagues who greeted me. "Tell us everything!" "What was your labor like?!" "Is she sleeping!?" "She looks *just* like you!" "How long are you here?" "Did you go into labor naturally?"

Needless to say, I was overstimulated with a capital "O." *Overstimulated!* Amidst the love I felt for these colleagues, I drew on my magical motherhood power of *thinking on my feet* and provided a general summary of my labor experience. Some of the guiding questions I asked myself included (1) What do I feel safe disclosing? (2) What self-preservation do I need in this moment? (3) How will I feel about this disclosure in ten minutes, ten days, or ten weeks? To address question number one, I was surrounded by colleagues who felt very safe. I chose to disclose *some* details of the labor and delivery without specific detail pertaining to my body, relational experience with my partner, and recovery. I shared timeframes of labor and delivery, a positive experience with the birthing center, and a few early delights of my daughter's personality. For question two, I knew I had about five minutes before reaching a point of complete overwhelm. I honored this time limit and then focused on one-on-one interactions with colleagues. For question three, I quickly assessed how I would feel about my disclosure (or lack thereof) in the immediate future (ten minutes), near future (ten days), and future (ten weeks). This final check-in helped me feel confident in the level of detail I decided to share.

Talking with hundreds of mothers over the years, specifically those transitioning back to work after having a baby, has provided ample opportunities to empathize with some of these questions and unsolicited comments made in the workplace. What I hear more often than not is how painful mothers find some of these questions, comments, and even microaggressions. Common questions and comments reported include:

Are you nursing?

What is your plan if your baby gets sick?

I keep forgetting you are a mom now!

Your pooch just looks like a beer belly now!

How do you manage to plan dinner?

You must be worried about missing out.

Do you ever worry about who is watching your baby?

It must be so nice to get a break from your baby!

Think twice if the thought has crossed your mind that this *could never happen to me.*

Question 1: "What is your plan if your baby gets sick?"

The mother who reported experiencing this question had a medically compromised child. Her immediate response was a feeling of pain, as she internally told herself, "*I am back at work and my baby IS sick.*" As tears streamed down her face, she experienced a secondary microaggression that evening at home, as her partner described the congratulatory responses of *his* colleagues, absent of any questions about childcare or *why* he had returned to work or *who* would now be cooking dinner.

Question 2: "Do you ever worry about who is watching your baby?"

The mother who was on the receiving end of this question had experienced debilitating separation anxiety. She had limited options when it came to childcare as she was a single mother without family nearby. Again, deeply painful. Yes, she was worried and was still building trust amidst pervasive separation anxiety. She responded with a short, terse statement as she knew she would lash out in rage (valid) or become flooded with tears. She also wondered if any of the dads in the office had been asked the same question. She didn't think so.

Comment 1: "It must be so nice to get a break from your baby!"

Once and for all, let us categorically set the record straight. Pulling a 5 a.m. to 10 p.m. double shift is *not* a break. In fact, while at work, many mothers carry the weight of work and the mental and emotional toll of motherhood *simultaneously. It. Is. Exhausting.* Similar to the mother in question two, this mother had also experienced separation anxiety, which led her to feel distress about coming to work; she did *not* experience her return as *a break.* Many mothers also feel as if they have worked a full day's work just from surviving the night, morning routine and childcare coordination.

Comment 2: "Your pooch just looks like a beer belly now!"

This mother was actually *me*. Body comments in the workplace are never okay. The silver lining in this interaction was that I had rapport with this person. He happened to work as an officer in the psychiatric department and *thought* he was giving me a compliment. I pulled him aside, shared that I did *not* feel comfortable with him commenting on my very postpartum mama pooch, and I am fairly confident that my eyes may have struck him with some form of electric shock! He profusely apologized and blamed his unfamiliarity with pregnancy and postpartum. Not an excuse, bud, but I think he received the message.

Additional ways to manage responses to inappropriate questions or unsolicited advice:

- First and foremost, it is *never* okay to comment on someone else's body in the workplace. *Period.*

- If you feel safe and rapport is intact with the individual, have a one-on-one conversation about their question or comment.

- If you need some time to formulate a response, that is *okay*. I recommend electronically documenting the interaction, then emailing yourself a copy. This will provide a timestamp and a description of the event. Momnesia is very real and important details can escape the best of us as time lapses.

- Repeat what the person just said. "Larry, you're asking me about the hours of my daughter's daycare?" More often than not, when I slowly reflected back an off comment, the other person caught him or herself and immediately self-corrected.

- If approaching the individual does not feel safe or productive, inform Human Resources. If you fear retaliation from the individual, be sure to include this in the complaint.

"For me, being a mother made me a better professional, because coming home every night to my girls reminded me what I was working for. And being a professional made me a better mother, because by pursuing my dreams, I was modeling for my girls how to pursue their dreams."

Michelle Obama

CALLING OUT WHEN BABY IS SICK

You are in the groove, everyone is starting to sleep again, and *wham* – baby spikes a fever at 3 a.m. Your next day is jam-packed with important meetings, and your partner's day looks just about the same. Perhaps you were up all night monitoring the fever and googling every possible diagnosis under the sun that includes *fever* as a symptom. Take a deep breath and keep on reading. Remember, you have done hard things, and you are about to continue to prove that you can continue to do hard things. Your baby will be *okay*. You will be *okay*. After breathing, and *more* breathing, conduct a little triage with your partner.

1. Before this scenario occurs, **set up a standing meeting with your partner on Sunday nights** (or the night before the beginning of the work week) to discuss your schedules. Should someone need to stay home, who is able to do so? If there is a particular day when you *both* have meetings or work obligations that cannot be changed, coordinate potential backup care, *in advance*. Notify that person(s) in advance so they are prepared to respond immediately.

2. **Use your child's medical support.** For example, if you need medical guidance about the severity of symptoms, possibility for contagiousness, or simply need clarity on medication dosage, your child's pediatrician should offer some type of nurse line triage.

3. Now is your time to **shine in your executive decision making, effective communication, and assertiveness.** Notify your work chain that you will be calling out. Whether you decide to disclose the reason is entirely up to you. If you decide to provide a reason, be clear and concise.

   i. *"My daughter has a high fever. I need to use sick leave."*

   ii. *"My son has immediate medical needs, so I will be taking him to the doctor today."*

   iii. *"I am caring for my child's medical needs today and will therefore arrive at work at noon instead of 8 a.m."*

4. **Provide a clear summary of your approach.** Email your chain of command and/or work team a clear summary of how you are approaching your sick day. This is another opportunity to demonstrate your ability to coordinate – with little notice (thanks, bebe) – your work obligations. This can also highlight your commitment to accomplishing your workload, even while physically absent.

   i. Begin with high priority tasks then work from there. How do you need to proceed?

   ii. Once you identify your plan, communicate it clearly to your chain of command and/or work team.

Here are some examples (note that none of them contain any apologetic language, just statements of fact):

"Hi team! I need to call out sick today to care for my child. I will be checking email intermittently but will not be able to guarantee a response until 5 p.m. I will be available for the 10 a.m. meeting via video conference, so please plan on my attendance."

"Good morning. I need to call out sick today. I have rescheduled all meetings for tomorrow afternoon. I will be responding to emails when in the office tomorrow."

"Hello all! I will be arriving late to work due to a medical appointment, at approximately 11 a.m. I plan to review notes from the 9 a.m. meeting upon my return."

5. ***Follow through***. Follow through with your plan and do not look back. Kick guilt to the curb. The meeting can wait. You will catch up on emails. Take care of your baby and take care of yourself.

PROTECTIONS AND RIGHTS. KNOWLEDGE IS POWER.

Knowledge is power when it comes to protecting yourself and your livelihood. More than ever, you have reason(s) to protect what you have worked so hard for. Protections and rights vary greatly depending on where you live in the world, so familiarizing yourself with the ones unique to you is an important first step. Think, for example, the juxtaposition between protections of the U.S. versus Scandinavia. Australia versus Africa. If reading this prior to giving birth, start the process now to equip yourself with knowledge of your protections and rights. If you are reading this *on* parental leave, it is *not* too late to familiarize yourself with your protections and rights. Common areas for use of protections and rights include (1) parental leave, (2) pregnancy-related disabilities, and (3) lactation/pumping in the workplace.

Guiding Principles

Although your rights and protections are going to look different depending on a variety of factors, including geographic location, workplace culture, and beyond, here are some guiding principles to help you best protect yourself. Appendix H also provides an exercise to help you identify macro and micro protections as well as limitations in each area.

Guiding principles:

1. ***Identify protective bodies.*** In the United States, for example, "The Patient Protection and Affordable Care Act (P.L. 111-148, known as the "Affordable Care Act") amended section 7 of the Fair Labor Standards Act ("FLSA") to require employers to provide "reasonable break time for an employee to express breast milk for her nursing child for one year after the child's birth each time such employee has need to express the milk." Employers are also required to provide "a place, other than a bathroom, that is shielded from view and free from intrusion from coworkers and the public, which may be used by an employee to express breast milk."

see 29 U.S.C. 2071.[29] This is one example of a federal law that can provide protection to you if you need to pump in the workplace. Another example is the American with Disabilities Act that protects women with a pregnancy-related disability from being terminated, demoted, or denied a promotion. For example, if you need extension of leave due to a postpartum mood disorder, you can use this protection. Smaller bodies of protection might include your human resources department (think policies and procedures unique to your place of employment), local advocacy groups, or unions associated with your workforce. My place of employment following my second parental leave had a designated lactation coordinator due to the large size of the agency. This was a helpful point of contact who provided agency specific guidance and advocacy. *MomsRising* is one organization that "takes on the most critical issues facing women, mothers, and families by educating the public and mobilizing massive grassroots actions." This platform, consisting of over a million members, can connect you with maternal and workplace justice education and support.

2.   *Identify limitations to these protections.* As straightforward as I wish motherhood were, this is another gray area full of limitations. Now is your time to identify such limitations in order to best navigate your transition back to the workplace. Let's examine the example of pumping protections. Perhaps your employer provides you a space *other than a bathroom,* akin to a closet, and this space is less than ideal for letdown, not to mention your very delicate mental health. What then? I wish this were not the case, but as I interviewed multiple women as research for this book, I heard *pumping places other than a bathroom* to include patient recovery rooms, storage rooms, and one woman even shared that her manager had suggested that she pump on public transportation so as not to disrupt a morning partner meeting. Another limitation is eligibility. Many women I interviewed were surprised to learn they had not met eligibility for *unpaid* (yes, *unpaid!*) protections under the "Family Medical Leave Act" due to either not having worked at their place of employment for a full year or not meeting the minimum of 1,250 work hours. If you are still pregnant, consider crunching numbers and strategize accordingly. Another common limitation repeated by many mothers interviewed was the one-year time limit to FLSA in regard to pumping rights. Many employers mimic this time-limit in their policy and procedures. Some women reported having received subtle comments surrounding *when* they intended on discontinuing lactation once they reached the one-year mark. Many experienced this questioning as a subtle reminder that this protection was coming to an end.

To these moms' stories of limitations, I can add my own. For my second parental leave I used the "Family Medical Leave Act." I crossed all of my t's and dotted all of my i's. My human resources representative confirmed that all of my paperwork had been adequately completed and approved. *Wahoo!* She then proceeded to outline the necessary requirements to initiate FMLA. She needed to know, *within 24 hours,* the delivery date and a variety of other extraneous details. Yes, amidst having a baby, I was to notify her that my baby had been born. *True story.* How inconceivable that women should be thinking about anything other than their cesarean wound or torn vagina, first postpartum poop, or baby who was just admitted to the NICU!

29   Wages and Hour Division. (2018). *Break time for nursing mothers under the FLSA.* United States Department of Labor. https://www.dol.gov/agencies/whd/fact-sheets/73-flsa-break-time-nursing-mothers

Yet, I feared if I did not have this prioritized among all that came with my delivery that my job would not be fully protected. Although FMLA is designed to be a supportive measure, the accompanying red tape can *add* needless anxiety.

3.   *Operationalize safeguards with newfound knowledge and circumstance.* Here comes the navigation piece. There is *a lot* of gray when it comes to decision making in motherhood. As I said before, multifactorial decision makings – one more skill to add to your resume. This final guiding principle is the integration of information surrounding your protections and rights, limitations of such, and your unique circumstances.

Example 1: Jennifer is a partner at her dental group. She meets the requirements for "Family Medical and Leave Act." However, patient availability is backing up and Jennifer is now receiving pressure from her partners to return after four weeks parental leave or forgo 75% of her salary. How would you proceed?

Example 2: Yvette has been diagnosed with D-MER, dysphoric milk ejection reflex, and has provided accompanying documentation to her human resources department. This is a highly sensitive topic for her and was asked by her human resources representative to identify reasonable accommodations. Although she could benefit from extended time to pump, she is uncomfortable navigating this topic with her manager. How would you proceed?

Think about (1) your protections and rights, (2) limitations to those protections and rights, and (3) how to best navigate and proceed in the healthiest way possible.

ADVOCATING FOR MORE

Advocating for what? More. More? How!? Hear me out. Having a baby does *not* equate to you losing interest in further developing your professional skills and competencies, contributing to collaborative projects, or leading ambitious endeavors. Most often unintentionally, supervisors and managers *assume* that you are disinterested in opportunities in any of the activities mentioned above.

"We figured you were too exhausted to take on anything else, so we asked Tony to take the lead."

"We needed someone who could stay beyond 6 p.m., and we know your son attends daycare."

"Maybe next year you would want to attend the conference? We know you have a lot on your plate."

If you want to develop professional skills and competencies, contribute to collaborative projects, or lead an ambitious endeavor, *ask*. Dispel any assumptions by your chain of command and *ask*. Once you ask, follow up and advocate for yourself.

LYNNE WRIGHT, SURGEON

Fertility Treatments, A High-Risk Pregnancy, Single Motherhood, and Pressure All Around

Lynne, as we will refer to her for anonymity, is a surgeon and single mother to a toddler son. Grab a box of tissues as her journey to motherhood will jerk tears from every eye duct. Due to the nature of her ambitious career, she saved eggs in her mid-30s. She and her partner began their conception journey at age 38, which unfortunately resulted in a miscarriage. This launched Lynne into infertility treatment due to her age. IUI was unsuccessful because of missed infection residual from her miscarriage, pivoting her to IVF. Between gruesome work schedules, Lynne and her partner traveled back and forth from the East to West Coast for IVF treatments. Her doctor was one of her best friends with whom she could just be a patient and not a doctor. Lynne underwent *four* retrievals. Her son, the only healthy embryo, was transferred into Lynne. Her partner, who was less adept at managing the emotional strain of fertility and their life, left Lynne when she was 17-weeks pregnant. By this time, Lynne had taken 500+ injections during this journey. Her parents moved in with Lynne to provide emotional and physical support as 60-hour weeks were the rule and not the exception.

At 26 weeks, the first glucose test came abnormal. Her mom sat with her at 28 weeks in the lab waiting area for three hours as she did the three-hour glucose test and passed. Phew! At 29 weeks pregnant she became febrile and, uncharacteristically, canceled two surgeries. That night she was on call when her brother (who was out of state) noted that she was shivering on the phone and told her to go to the ER. She had driven herself to and from the ER since her mom was unfamiliar with the roads (and her father had just left them temporarily for some work out of state). She was diagnosed with Influenza A and found to be contracting every four hours. She was prescribed immediate bedrest.

Two days later came the pressure from her medical partners. "Lynne, when are you coming back?" Five days later, her partners (parents of two, three, and four children respectively) asked her to not take a paycheck. One of her partners, a mother of four children, stated "I had to do it so you should too." This statement caused Lynne deep pain, especially hearing this from a female colleague and *mother*. Instead of a follow up sentence involving copious curse words – which would have been valid – Lynne gently said, "Becky, we should become *kinder*. We should *strive* to make the world a better place." Lynne could have thrown her hands up, at any one of these traumas, and ran for the woods. What struck me was her utmost gentleness, forgiveness, and resilience.

Despite prescription of bedrest, she returned to the office at 34 weeks pregnant and delivered at 39 weeks. "How did you survive, Lynne?" I asked.

"Becky, I did not have a choice. I am not religious, but I have faith in a higher power, and I prayed every night for my son and my family. I didn't have control, and I needed to relinquish control. Be strategic, ride the wave, and keep perspective."

Mental and physical trauma continued following her cesarean section. For example, the night after her cesarean section, while at the hospital, she asked the nursery to tend to her son so she could rest and recover from surgery, making the common request from a first-time mom to refrain from offering him a pacifier. Within a few minutes, the nurse brought her son back to Lynne. "If you won't agree to a pacifier, he is not our problem. Here."

Despite having experienced a traumatic entrance to motherhood, she leaned on her support system, which included friends and family. She had three baby showers thrown for her from three sets of friends with an outpouring of gifts and well-wishes. Lynne knew, without a shadow of a doubt, that she and her son were loved. Leaning on her support system transformed into necessity as challenges persisted. Her son became jaundiced, which required integrating formula. At three weeks old he had a choking episode requiring EMT intervention. The sight of her son blue is an image tattooed on her hippocampus. Her son choked a *second* time at four weeks old when Lynne started chest compressions right before EMT came to the rescue again. Thank God for them! "All my medical knowledge had no meaning at that moment as a helpless mom." After this he was monitored in the hospital for two nights and diagnosed with reflux. Lynne developed mastitis during his hospitalization and returned to work the following week.

Remember those tissues? You might want to grab one. Another area of resilience was her ability to forge ahead and perform six to seven surgeries per day, all while continuing to pump. Lynne pumped in recovery rooms, locker rooms, and random empty rooms – in between surgeries, which consisted of a ten-minute break! "At times I would get called in the middle of a pump. I would cry." Regardless, she developed a well-organized pumping system, which she later imparted to some of her nursing staff.

Lynne recommended that mothers use help – nannies, parents, friends, sleep consultants – and emphasized that there is no *ego* in accepting second-hand items. She also encouraged mothers using family support to keep perspective. "There are pluses and minuses. I needed the help." She also recommended sleep training sooner rather than later as well as holding onto the *amazing, fun,* and *joyous* moments. "In surgical training we have a saying, 'the beatings will continue until the morale improves.' I feel life has given me my share of beatings, but I am constantly reminding myself, look what I have! He is growing up to be a wonderfully happy boy. I am excited to build my life with him."

IDENTIFY GAPS. EXECUTE CHANGE.

Someday we will live in a world where employers have mastered the art of supporting parents during this major life transition. For now, when we identify a gap (or gaps), the best we can do is advocate change. Where we encounter individuals or cultures that have low empathy, we can model and encourage more *compassion* and *gentleness*. When we feel isolated, under-resourced and under-supported, we can *create a work group of working parents*. If Human Resources omits pertinent information surrounding return from parental leave, we can *educate them*. If there is no policy or procedure surrounding teleworking or flex-scheduling, we can *create one*. Let us develop solutions, not ruminate on problems. The more we engage with our surrounding environments, the more likely they will come to reflect our values and respond to our needs. Employed mothers rule the world.

Join with Human Resources

Not all human resources departments are created equally, nor saturated with experts in the transition to employed motherhood. Some smaller companies might not even have an actual department but a single HR point of contact. This might be another gap you identify requiring you to execute change. Some potential scenarios you might encounter are (1) your HR department is limited in their knowledge in this area, (2) you *are* HR (i.e., self-employed) and/or (3) your role interfaces *often* with HR as either a manager or you work in HR.

The American Psychiatric Association's Center for Workplace Mental Health[30] outlines several tools and strategies for employers specifically to support mothers experiencing perinatal mood and anxiety disorders that are relevant to other pregnancy-related disabilities or even parental burnout or subclinical depression or anxiety. The Center for Workplace Mental Health suggests that HR:

1. Know what to look for

2. Help promote earlier screening

3. Prioritize sharing information

4. Make sure that employees know their rights

5. Calculate the feasibility of providing extended, or even paid, parental leave.

---

30   Kuhl, E. A. (n.d.). Tools and strategies to combat peripartum and postpartum depression and anxiety in working mothers. *Center for Workplace Mental Health.* https://workplacementalhealth.org/Mental-Health-Topics/Postpartum-Depression-and-Anxiety

Create a Telework or Flexible Schedule Option

If a policy does not already exist in the realm of remote or hybrid schedules (which in today's world would seem rather surprising!),create one. If feasible in your line of work, make this very intense life transition a little bit easier. Kick all of those "what if" fears and limiting beliefs, get out of your own way, and make this happen.

Here are some tips to support you in this process:

1. **Research. Then research some more.** Establish a leg to stand on. A common mistake is when an employee tries to make a proposal without having researched even the company's own current or recently updated policy. Read carefully through telework and flexible scheduling policy and procedure. If you are struggling to find it, contact human resources. There are new bodies of research in support of telework and flexible scheduling as bolstering productivity not the inverse. Be prepared to provide concrete evidence. You can also collect anecdotal evidence of co-workers who have negotiated a telework or flexible schedule.

2. **Create a proposal. Assertively highlight the positives.** Identify your ideal and align those with your employer's needs. Would your ideal look like two telework days but important in-person meetings falling on three days per week? This might be a thoughtful segue into acknowledging your employer's needs (presenting in-person for those meetings three days per week) and *your* need to work the other days remotely. The other consideration is flexing your schedule. For example, those wellness visits come often, especially the first year of life. On days when you have immunizations scheduled, you might want to monitor your child for reactions or keep him home for the remainder of the day for additional rest. If you have exhausted your leave, could the hours used for the wellness visit be made up throughout the week? This is one example of when having a conversation surrounding flexible scheduling with management – in advance – can alleviate future stress and angst. Lastly, assertively highlight the positives, including your increased productivity during remote working days (i.e., ability to log in early sans commute, uninterrupted focus, access to virtual meeting participation) and your commitment to meeting the needs of the employer.

3. **Strategically identify a time to discuss with your manager.** Now is the time to thoughtfully strategize the timing of this conversation, a conversation that deserves concerted focus. Instead of broaching the topic at the end of an informal check-in, request a time to meet face-to-face with your manager. Think about the most strategic time when competing priorities will be minimized. For example, if you know your manager has back-to-back intense meetings all day Thursday, you might want to avoid Thursday afternoons.

4. ***Ask.*** This is when you hear my gentle voice say, "Breathe. You have got this. Breathe." Refrain from diarrhea of the mouth and breathe. Now is the time to present your well developed, thoughtful proposal. Make eye contact, do *not* apologize, and hold yourself back from venting about *why* you desperately need a telework and flexible scheduling option. Your manager does not need to know how your daily commute eats into your

precious time with your little one or how this would allow for you to integrate a walk into your lunch break to maintain your physical and mental health. You do not need to provide an explanation. Asking is enough. You can do it. Breathe and stay positive.

5. **If the answer is *no*.** If you receive an automatic *no*, do not panic. This is an opportunity to demonstrate your spectrum of professional skills further refined through motherhood. Request a specific timeframe to revisit the conversation and verbalize your optimistic approach to a follow-up discussion. Offer to provide a written memo surrounding your conversation as well as some of your findings on the positive impact of productivity through remote and flexible scheduling avenues.

6. **Consider changing jobs.** Remote / hybrid work is here to stay. It's a filter on job search engines, so if you need it: use it. A quick search on "best remote companies" will yield you lists of hundreds of options. There are also websites (like fairygodboss.com) that provide insider information about company culture, to give you more peace of mind about where you are going to be landing.

Create Support

During this season of life, we *all* need as much support as possible. If it does not already exist in your place of employment, forming an employed parental support group can provide a built-in support system *in* your workplace. For all you know, your colleague two doors down has been considering it for years but has not had the wherewithal – for good reasons – to get the ball rolling.

Here is a general guideline for building a parental support group in your place of employment:

Step 1: Formulate and Formalize Your Mission.

Defining the mission is an integral first step. The last thing an employed mother, or parent for that matter, wants to do is spend precious time participating in a group that does not serve them well. Am I right? As employed mothers, we have to judiciously allocate our time and energy. Define the mission accordingly. Is your goal to have an education/resourced focus group? A safe space for employed parents to vent? A monthly meeting to bring in inspirational speakers? Define the mission so that very busy, exhausted mothers and parents know what they are signing up for. Secondly, once you have defined the mission of the group, present it to human resources. They can formalize the group and offer supportive resources.

Step 2: Do not recreate the wheel. *Do* lean into what is working.

No doubt there are internal resources readily accessible. Find them. They are there. Sure, maybe they could use a tune up, but there is no need to recreate the wheel if you do not have to. If there is a nursing room in your place of employment, highlight this resource. If there are ways to improve the nursing space, great, but there is no need to start from scratch. If there is a point of contact within Human Resources who is well versed in all policies relevant to employed parents of young children, consider asking this person to speak at one of the meetings instead of hiring someone externally. It might surprise you just *how* many resources lready exist in your place of employment; you just have to identify them.

Step 3: Keep it real, relatable, and solution focused.

As therapeutic as it can be for crispy fried parents to vent about *all the things* relating to employed parenthood, keep the tone constructive. At the same time, stay mindful that just because all of your members are parents, does not mean they all have the same problems to solve – or that they all have the means to solve the problem in the same way. Sure, the senior manager is a new parent. This person *might* be an ally, but if she spends hours speaking about how to hire an au pair or the ins-and-outs of managing a nanny, this might not resonate with employees struggling to find safe, reliable daycare without breaking the bank. Consider topics and resources that *all* can benefit from, not just the employee sitting in the corner office.

Step 4: Educate members about benefits and resources.

Many mothers I interviewed reported feeling too exhausted to even sort through all of the different benefits and resources newly available to them. It became *overwhelming* and *intimidating* to sort through the complex nuances of dependent care flexible spending, 529 plans, and the medical grade breast pump that was allegedly free via their health benefits. Providing clear, approachable material on benefits and resources can increase the likelihood that employed parents will access them. One approach might be to break into small groups to exchange tips and tricks for accessing these resources in efficient ways. For example, one mother I interviewed laughed as she described her journey of mastering uploading of dependent care receipts via an app on her phone as a monthly ritual on her commute home on the train.

SHANNON BARTLETT

Finding Self-Compassion During a Bumpy Transition

Shannon works full-time as a Real Estate Analyst and is the mother to a beautiful three-year-old son. Interviewing Shannon highlighted a common phenomenon that women experience during the transition to motherhood: an initial influx of negative, intrusive self-talk that slowly transforms into positive affirmations and self-compassion when they realize the sheer impossibility of achieving perfection during this major life transition. Shannon's journey to employed motherhood is no exception. Shannon's son suffered from severe acid reflux. Consistent with the diagnosis, he required around-the-clock care. Shannon and her partner tag-teamed the night shift.

After months of chronic sleep deprivation and deteriorating mental health, they knew that something had to change, at least temporarily. Shannon described her intense negative self-talk as the little voice that would tell her to *do* something instead of offering self-compassion and self-health. Shannon and her partner finally decided to sit down and discuss how a *temporary* transition to part-time work would impact their family. Shannon described this process with her partner as difficult yet compassionate. They found solace in finding the budget items to slash in order to make a temporary transition for Shannon to work part-time. A simple pro-con list provided them adequate clarity surrounding not only the financial perspective but also the benefit of Shannon's physical and mental well-being. The concrete list provided a logical viewpoint, rather than basing their decision making in emotional reactivity. She developed strategies to quiet the little voice telling her to "go do a load of laundry" and replace it with "Be nice to yourself. You need to sleep. Just chill."

To plant the seed for her request to go part time, Shannon communicated directly with her manager. For example, she professionally disclosed her son's medical diagnosis and the impact on her overall functioning a few weeks prior to her request. Resolutely, she whispered at this point of the interview, *"Becky, people are people before professionals."* She leaned into her newly developed motherhood creativity and identified a part-time position within her existing company that aligned with her personal needs and professional goals. "In the grand scheme of life, it is such a small window."

"I can't believe
we do this.
we are amazing".

-SHANNON BARTLETT-

Fast forward to now, and Shannon has made a transition back to full-time employment. She emphasized the importance of ongoing self-compassion and self-health. Shannon described her current daily commute as her *me-time*, which includes listening to podcasts, calling loved ones, and stopping at the gym three to four times per week to break up her travel time. She continues to pursue her professional goals in industrial real estate and has never been more in love with her son and partner.

WHEN YOUR FIELD IS INSATIABLE

Conducting my research for this book introduced me to a theme amongst women within certain fields. *Burnout*. When I examined some of the trends amongst these women, I found a common thread that led to the conclusion that all of these women were employed in a field with, as Tracey Jensen most eloquently describes it, "insatiable appetites for time and energy." The most obvious field of work with an insatiable appetite for time and energy is ostensibly motherhood, no? Compound this with a line of work that is also insatiable, and you have designed the perfect recipe for burnout. Are you in an insatiable field? Jensen said it best. "Both motherhood and academia [or any insatiable field] have appetites for time and energy, both saturated with toxic fantasies of effortless perfection."

When you are operating in not one but *two* insatiable fields, it is critical to (1) **define *your* enough** and (2) **implement and *reinforce* healthy, clear, and realistic boundaries.** Easier said than done, I know; it can often feel that working mothers are facing a kind of institutional gaslighting. Policy expert Clair Clark and sociologist Sally Gallagher present the dilemma at the heart of their findings in this way: "While our institutions have put in place family‑friendly employment policies, and make use of equity rhetoric, the reality is that, as long as the institutional demand for our product is limitless, the unencumbered worker continues to be the ideal."[31] Earlier in this book we covered our many roles as well as internal/external expectations. Clark and Gallagher's words, although no less than a sucker punch, are a reminder of all of the internal/external pressures experienced as an employed mother. If we are going to thrive as such, we must equip ourselves with the skills to define our *enough* and set healthy boundaries.

Defining enough

This is the time to have a heart-to-heart with yourself. "What is *my* enough?" In motherhood. In your profession. Then, operationalize this into everyday life. For me, I worked backward. For example, I identified my annual revenue goal for my practice and matched it to the number of clients I could manage. From there, I crunched some numbers, solidified cost per session to meet my annual goal, and blessed my plan after confirming that my numbers were aligned with market value. In other words, I could justify that hourly rate with my market value. From there, I crystallized some daily benchmarks specifically in the realm of mother-daughter(s) interactions. Some examples included daily one-on-one reading time for *at least* 15 minutes (anything beyond was a bonus), 30 minutes of mindful, individualized quality time (typically spent on the floor relishing in all of their amazingness), and daily family dinners. This was *my* enough that served to inform my daily habits and routines.

---

31   Clark, C., & Gallagher, S. K. (2017). The influence of state maternity leave policies on US mothers' employment. *Community, Work & Family, 20*(4), 459–478. https://doi.org/10.1080/13668803.2016.1227769

Setting healthy boundaries and limits

Protecting your *enough* is the next step. I am here to gently warn you that these boundaries and limits will be tested, then pushed, then pushed some more. Do. Not. Budge. Protect your boundaries and set healthy limits. The work call can wait.

Here are some words of wisdom I learned along the way:

1. **Define your work hours and communicate them.** If you are in the office from 9 a.m.–5 p.m. Monday–Friday, own it. You are there for eight solid hours to produce and provide intentional, quality working time. Let others know that these are your working hours and communicate them accordingly. Reinforce as needed. One tip I heard during one of my interviews was assertively attaching working hours in her email template, below her signature. Brilliant, no? Establishing a clear schedule will not only provide you structure and predictability – something you might desperately be craving for during this season – but will also provide it for your child, partner, childcare provider, and employer. To echo the sage Katie Couric, "Get rid of the guilt. When you're at one place, don't feel bad that you're not at work; when you're at work, don't feel bad that you're not at home."

2. **Follow through.** If you set a boundary and then only partially reinforce it, the result (based on what we know from rat studies) is severe anxiety and hair loss – two things no mom needs more of! If you say you are leaving work at 5 p.m., leave work at 5 p.m. If your child routinely reads with you each night, provide that consistently and reliability. To this day, my daughter gravitates to the kitchen table at 5:30 p.m. and turns off her tablet in preparation for our electronics-free meal. This is no coincidence, but years of consistent dinner times integrated as a daily family ritual.

3. **Say no by saying yes.** This is one of my best kept secrets, the art of saying no by saying yes. It might sound something like this:

"Yes! I look forward to discussing those points tomorrow when I am in the office. Does 10 a.m. work for you?"

"I am eager to solidify plans for the conference as well! We make a great team. I would love to set something up for Monday since my day ends today at 5 p.m."

4. **Radical acceptance.** You are human. You are *one* person. You are *enough*. Putting in a solid eight hours of work is *enough*. Mindfully playing on the floor for 20 beautiful minutes with your child is *enough*.

Dimension of Wellness: Social

NOTES

CHAPTER 8

SOCIAL WELLNESS

It takes a village to raise a child. Ways to build your tribe.

umans are social creatures. There is a reason why we continue to need one another, even in a time when technologies and conveniences are at an all-time high. A study in Clinical Psychological Science discovered that stress hormones actually foreshadow postpartum depression in new mothers, strong support, specifically from family members, seemed to protect mothers from developing postpartum depression. Although research still needs to back this up, I believe that it is a fair generalization to assume that a strong support system can serve as a protective factor amongst many disorders and increase the likelihood of a smooth transition to employed motherhood.

Try to imagine undergoing this transition sans support. What would that be like? When you visualize your *people,* who comes to mind? Who do you wish lived closer? Whose presence do you experience comfort from? In this section, we will explore (1) your relationship with your child, (2) the relationship with those caring for your child, (3) how to establish a new contract with your partner, (4) tips for partners, (5) how to establish and maintain friendships specifically with other moms, and (5) ways to coordinate paid support.

YOUR RELATIONSHIP WITH YOUR CHILD

Out of the frying pan and into the fire. That is how many of the women I interviewed described their transition back to the office. One minute you are spending every waking hour – for months even – relishing and soaking in every smell, milestone, and coo, the next you are spending 50–60 hours away from your baby. This is a *big shift* not only for you, but also for your baby. Acknowledging that this *is* an adjustment can ease some of the pressure to maintain what once was. To manage this evolving relationship, engage in mindful interactions when you *are* with your baby to *catch back up.* Keep in mind, babies do not need a lot. *But* they *do* need love, connection, and security. These are all things you can provide as an employed mother. You *can* do both. I learned a slew of tips and tricks to pass on to *you* that helped me in maintaining a close, connected, and secure relationship with my baby.

Invite your baby into your world of employment

Your worlds do not have to exist separately. They can coexist and intersect. You might have occasion to bring your baby into the workplace (or have her brought to you by the caregiver), your baby might pop into an occasional video call because you work from home, or you might call your baby from work. This is what I did while working in an emergency department, I somehow found an empty interview room to video-call my baby. As she grew into a toddler, this became an organic opportunity to introduce her to doctors and police officers. One evening when my daughter struggled to fall asleep, I remember an officer overhearing me quietly singing to her and snuck in the room to join me. This meant the world to me and, no doubt, made me the coolest mom in the world at a time when I was all-consumed with guilt for not being able to snuggle her to sleep physically.

Another way to introduce her into your world of employment is through books. I found some books at the library with either characters or themes in line with my career that allowed for natural opportunities for me to explain to her what I did when I was away. She developed an appreciation and eventually asked me for daily debriefings of *how* I was a *helper* today. *Tell* your baby about your day, even if it feels silly or you do not believe your baby can comprehend. Several studies suggest that a child's receptive language is well developed by just six months old. You can also tell them how much you miss them and think about them throughout the day. Even though they may not fully understand, the positive effect of interpersonal neurobiology will indubitably replenish you with oxytocin.

Intentional mindful moments

Mindful moments can facilitate reconnection while separated during the week. For me, mindful moments came in many forms: **mirroring** and **mimicking, talking, rituals** and **music**. Mirroring and mimicking your baby might include mirroring his facial expressions or mimicking her coos. No matter how silly this might feel, this is an exercise that will facilitate your connection. Meet those sweet baby eyes and mirror away.

You may not think of your baby as a conversationalist but give it a try and you may find that you're communicating on a deep level. Talk to your baby. Tell them about your day, stories about your life, and narrate those precious moments together. "I am here with you *right* now and there is nowhere I would rather be!" *Reading* is another avenue of communicating with your baby that is never too early to start. Each night before bedtime we read *Guess How Much I Love You,* which became a conversation starter for all things love. *Why* I love her, moments during my workday I felt love for her, and *how* my love continued to grow for her.

Positive rituals might come where you least expect them. One of the routines I always despised with my first was daycare drop off. Despite the efforts spent the night before to ensure that nothing could go wrong (doesn't that sound like I am already jinxing myself?), something catastrophic would seem to occur just as we were headed to the car. Okay, maybe what happened just *felt* catastrophic. Applesauce or the lovely projectile spit up, remembering the diaper bag when we were nearly to her daycare, realizing that my breast pump was missing an essential part. I learned to adjust the baseline of drop off and accepted the potential for something to go awry. As I embraced this new mindset, I found small rituals at the start of our day. For example, each time I buckled baby girl, I made it a point to touch her nose, kiss her cheeks, and tell her how much I loved her. As she got older, she loved to press the car lock, which became another ritual after exiting the car. These simple but meaningful rituals became moments for intentional, mindful connection.

Music is a powerful connecting tool. You do not have to be a professional singer or musician to draw upon music for connection. Musically inclined or tone deaf, use this powerful tool to connect with your little one. Blast some upbeat music and dance, rest with some classical music, or share a part of yourself with some music from your past. *Connect.*

As my daughter started to comprehend and experience intense separation anxiety, we incorporated a song from the book *The Kissing Hand* by Audrey Penn. We created a hand itual and sang *The Kissing Hand*, which continued for months until it became a distant memory. This was a mechanism for safety not only for her, but me as well. On days *I* was experiencing separation anxiety, I hummed that sweet song and felt comfort. Still today, at seven, she creatively incorporates some mechanism when she experiences separation anxiety; our babyhood rituals helped her internalize a coping strategy that continues to serve her well.

SELECTING CHILD CARE RIGHT FOR *YOU*

I unabashedly admit that my understanding of childcare was myopic before becoming a mother. How I was wrong, and never happier to be so. If I could impart just one modicum of wisdom in this area, it would be that childcare is fluid and impermanent. If something is not working, you can re-evaluate and pivot. Nothing is set in stone and you can adapt your childcare to your family's ever-evolving needs. To get started, familiarize yourself with the various childcare options available to you.

Here are a few different types of childcare.

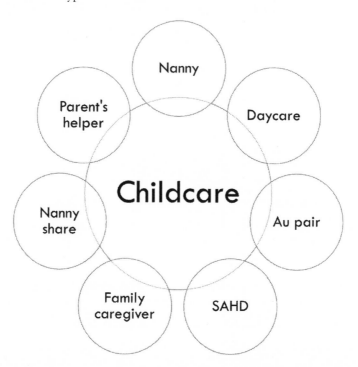

As you look at your various options, remember that you can access more than one. There are endless combinations depending on the needs of your family. For example, if a family member is able to watch your child two days per week, you can find a part-time childcare option to supplement. If your partner works part-time odd hours, a nanny share might make more sense. If you work long hours that fluctuate or you travel often, hiring a nanny or au pair with increased flexibility might be the way to go. Find what works best for *you*.

Trust that you know what you and your family needs. Your family's childcare needs are unique and deserve an individualized approach as no one-size-fits-all exists in the world of childcare. Be kind and gentle with yourself. If you need to re-evaluate because the current child care situation is not working, then pause and launch where you need to launch. You have got this.

THE RELATIONSHIP WITH YOUR CHILDCARE PROVIDER

The relationship with your childcare provider is one like no other: intimate yet saturated with boundaries, familiar but ever full of nuance. This was a learning curve that took me through a few different ups and downs before I understood the dance. Be patient with yourself, your baby, and your childcare provider as you all establish trust and a working relationship.

Communication

Communication is the key to any good relationship, is it not? Now is the time to over-communicate and, as you will tell your toddler at some point, "Use your words!" Seriously, this will prevent sliding down a rabbit hole of mindreading and assumptions. In this section we will cover the importance of *establishing expectations* and *debriefings*.

Establish expectations

This is a process to start at the onset and one to thoughtfully marinate in prior to moving forward with a provider. Expectations protect you, your child, the provider, and the overall relationship. First and foremost, what *are* your expectations surrounding childcare? How can you clearly broach a conversation surrounding these expectations? In the coming pages I provide a summary constructed by Childcare.gov that you can use as a guide for identifying some of your expectations of your quality childcare provider.

Here is what I recommend:

1. **Start from scratch.** Brainstorm with your partner what exactly you expect from a childcare provider. Write this down and revise as you reevaluate.

2. When exploring a potential avenue for childcare, **inquire about their existing policies**. If they have a handbook, ask for a copy. Carefully read through the handbook and ask informative questions. If there is a particular approach they subscribe to, seek understanding about how this approach is actually operationalized.

3. **Identify gray areas and seek clarification.** If *you* are the one creating the handbook, for example, in the case of a nanny, carefully address the gray areas. Remember, these are working documents and childcare providers are *typically* receptive to feedback surrounding their policies or adapting such to meet a specific family need.

*Some common gray areas include storage of breastmilk, time frame when frozen milk is considered expired and subsequently disposed, caregiver kissing children or verbalizing *I love you*, policy surrounding late pickup in the case of traffic, disclosure of milestones, documentation and communication of minor injuries, enforcement of sick policies (what symptoms will result in your child needing to be sent home, what is required for them to be able to return to school), COVID notifications, and weather or health-related shut-downs.

Milestones don't exist until MAMA sees them!

Debriefings

Debriefings are the invisible string between you and your child. These are integral at both the morning handoff *and* evening pickup. Yes, these are periods of high stress. I have shown up to my daughter's daycare center or been greeted by our nanny only to realize how *late* I was or that I had neglected mascara on one eye. Alas, take a moment to debrief the caregiver. A guiding checklist might include:

1. **Sleep.** How did your baby sleep last night? Was the sleeping routine *status quo* or is there anything to report in terms of anticipating an early nap or potential transition in amount of daytime sleep?

2. **Feeding schedule.** When will the first feeding take place? Did your little one cluster-feed all night? Do you anticipate your baby requiring an extra feed due to a growth spurt?

3. **Behavior.** Any changes in behavior to report? Teething perhaps? Extra clinginess and need for snuggles?

4. **Diapering.** It might sound silly, but there *will* be a day when the handoff includes last night's diaper. It is *okay*. Let them know and move on. Another consideration is change in bowel movements or urination, color, frequency, smell, etc. Let them know as this can be helpful information.

5. **Routine.** Was there a change in the routine? Did Aunt Sally make a surprise visit and overstimulate your baby well beyond bedtime? Is your partner away for travel? Take some time to report any routine changes.

ncorporate Positivity

.eep perspective that childcare is hard work for little pay. Be kind to those caring for your •aby. This is also a job most often outsourced to *women*. Sit in that for a moment. Let us upport other women as they support us and our little ones. A small token of gratitude, such s a heart-felt *thank you* or small gift card with a handwritten note can mean the world.

)ffer the benefit of the doubt

his is a hard one. If you witness or hear about something that sounds off, *breathe*. Then, •reathe again. Offer the benefit of the doubt prior to assuming the worst. I regret not having vritten down the slew of situations I had negatively perceived or overreacted to, only to umbly reassemble my cognitive/emotional framework once I had all of the details. While the letails have long since evaporated, the opportunity to practice reframing (remember section ?) and assertive communication continue to translate back to the office.

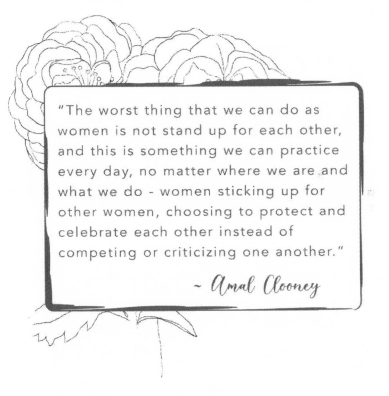

"The worst thing that we can do as women is not stand up for each other, and this is something we can practice every day, no matter where we are and what we do - women sticking up for other women, choosing to protect and celebrate each other instead of competing or criticizing one another."

~ Amal Clooney

Childcare.gov has a wealth of resources for all things childcare. Below is a list of *what you can expect* from a quality childcare provider, which can serve as a metric for *your* childcare search.

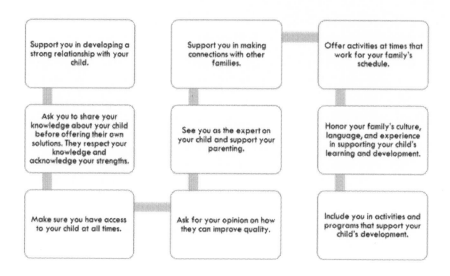

ESTABLISHING A NEW CONTRACT WITH YOUR PARTNER

The growing pains of this life transition affects all of the joints and muscles. Your relationship with your partner is no exception. *Most* couples report some form of strain on their relationship after having a baby, so you are not alone. Do not be fooled by all of the social media highlight reels. Trust that the stress that your relationship feels is not abnormal or atypical by any stretch. As an employed mom and partner who has transitioned *twice* and – by no short of a miracle – is still in love (seriously) with her partner, I promise that this season will soon be a distant memory. It is a *season,* not a forever. Be kind to each other. Be gentle. Be forgiving. Support and love one another, even when you want nothing else but to scream or run far, far away.

Topics to discuss with your partner in preparation for your return to work:

- **Sleep:** If you've been doing more of the night feedings because you've been on leave, nip that recipe for resentment in the bud and renegotiate how you will handle nights now that you're back at work. (Even if you're breastfeeding, you can find ways to get your partner to help out, like bringing you the baby; you can also use some of your pumped milk and have them do a nighttime bottle feed.)

- **Housework:** Are there tasks that need to be eliminated, outsourced or reassigned to your partner?

- Daycare illnesses: Plan in advance for those one-off super challenging nights. Be on the same page *before* your congested baby is up all night resisting sleep training. If you present a united front, you'll avoid adding fuel to the fire.

- Work boundaries: Whose day ends when? Is one of you always in charge of drop off and pickup? Who is on call for emergencies? If those roles are fluid, how will you decide who does what and when?

- Alone / recharge / self-care time: How will your return to work impact each of your individual routines? Things like getting physical activity, social time, naps, etc., should be part of the discussion so you each make sure to refill your cup in a way that doesn't drain the other person's.

Communication

If communication is a strength of your partnership, celebrate away! If not, rest assured that you are amongst good company. *Most* couples struggle with communication. This is an opportunity to practice. One common challenge I help couples with during this major life transition is how to communicate about the full spectrum of thoughts and feelings, not solely the positive. Communicate about the good, the bad, and the ugly, even if this feels vulnerable and unfamiliar. Practicing these skills as a couple will provide the foundation for years to come as you navigate future life transitions.

Here are some communication strategies to employ:

1. **Use a script to practice healthy communication.** Remember those I-Feel statements? This is an opportune time to practice turning your thoughts and feelings into an I-Feel statement. Once one person shares an I-Feel statement, the other person reflects on it. After reflective listening, offer validation and empathy.

Partner 1: "I am feeling discouraged and abandoned when I have asked repeatedly for help during the night feeding. I need you to follow through on your promise to help me at night."

Partner 2: "I hear you. You are saying that you feel discouraged and abandoned when I have not helped during night feedings when I have promised to. Your feelings make sense, and I can see how you would feel that way. Moving forward, I am going to show up."

2. **Resist assumptions or mindreading.** When stressed, tired, or triggered, it is easy to run down the rabbit hole of assuming *how* someone is thinking or feeling. It is also easy to try to read someone else's mind instead of processing your own thoughts and feelings and then finding the words to express them. Resist the urge; before jumping to conclusions, inquire about what the other person is thinking and feeling.

3. **Overcommunicate.** Overcommunicate. Overcommunicate. Overcommunicate. In this busy season of life, in order to keep the countless moving parts from getting stuck, you need to grease the gears by sharing information – and lots of it. Consider this another valuable characteristic to add to your resume – triage queen. Whether it be debriefing your partner during a handoff, updating the family calendar app with an upcoming pediatrician appointment, or providing context to what is contributing to your increased emotionality, communicate it. Your partner cannot know what they do not know.

4. **When in doubt, clarify.** Before reacting, clarify what the other person is saying. A little bit of curiosity goes a long way.

5. **Establish rituals.** Establishing rituals can offer predictable and consistent opportunities to communicate. Block out time if needed. My partner and I tried (yes, we missed a Friday or two) to block out time after our girls went to bed on Fridays to talk about our needs and expectations over the weekend. On Sundays, we briefly sat down and discussed what the upcoming week looked like. Albeit imperfectly, we tried to sprinkle in acknowledgements of *wins* and what we did well as parents, which was always a nice dopamine hit.

6. **Communication comes in many forms.** Use technology to your advantage. Communication does *not* need to look a certain way. Depending on your unique circumstances, it might come in the form of texting, video calls, emails, phone applications, and beyond. Identify and then utilize what works best for you all as a partnership.

Defensiveness

A pattern of defensiveness is a sure proof path to unhappiness, attorney fees, and wasted time and energy. As a relational therapist, I believe this is one of the most challenging areas to address in the therapy room as it is *often* the result of a longstanding guard against deep fears of losing control or being abandoned. If defensiveness pops up for you when communicating with your partner, examine it, dissect it, and identify the root cause. From there, tolerate any discomfort that arises when you make yourself vulnerability and slow your brain down enough to *really* hear your partner. Use the script above if needed and trust the process. If you get stuck, hire a professional to help you and/or your partner.

I-Feel Statement: "I feel worried and stressed about my first day back to work on Monday. There is so much change coming next week."

Defensive Response: "You don't need to feel worried. Do you not think I will support you? It is going to be fine. You just need to be more positive."

Reflective, Validating Response: "I hear that you are worried and stressed about Monday. It *is* a lot of change. How can I best support you?"

Do you hear the difference? Try practicing these tools in moments of calm in order to practice for the big game.

Division of Household Labor

Managing a household, coupled with child rearing and employment, is not for the faint of heart. This is one of those examples when I would sprinkle in a joke about mom not being an octopus. Truly, everyone, I *only* have two hands and *one* brain. As you and your partner find your rhythm in this transition, this is one more area to healthily tackle – *division of household labor.*

Here are some recommendations:

1. **Technology is your friend.** As much as I value good old-fashioned paper and pen, technology meets this season's need for pace and efficiency. My partner and I used a spreadsheet system, a living document, which was accessible via cloud. We identified each category of household labor then listed each item, big and small. In the adjacent column we identified who was in charge of each task. Other helpful uses of technology included a project management smartphone app, which we transitioned to after realizing the helpfulness of our spreadsheet system. We also used another smartphone app as our shared family calendar, which was a lifesaver, particularly in communicating to the other when a future appointment was created. For example, my partner scheduled my daughter's four-month appointment at her three-month visit. When I saw the date via alert on the smartphone app, I knew to block out my work calendar for that time period as we alternated between who took our daughter to each wellness visit.

2. **Integrate visual reminders.** With our spreadsheet system, we printed a master copy and placed it on the fridge. Once we fully transitioned to smartphone apps (primarily a project management app and shared family calendar), we subscribed to the alerts and reminders. As much as I like to believe that I consistently check the calendar, there was more than one occasion when I had to do some last-minute rearranging as I had not anticipated the appointment or event.

3. **When/if feasible, outsource.** Hands down, this is the best money I spend every month. This was not always something that we could afford, and really had to get over our own guilt in accessing this *luxury* as neither my partner nor I had grown up with outsourcing. We pushed through the guilt and never looked back. If you can find a way to budget for even a monthly deep cleaning, *do it.* Amidst all of the chaos and lack of control this season of life brings, walking through the door to a clean house just brings a moment of peace worth its weight in gold.

TIPS FOR PARTNERS

1. **Be a source of comfort and support.** Let your guard down and check any defensiveness. Like many women transitioning back to work, she spent ten months pregnant attaching to her child, then familiarized herself with spending the days with her baby. *Now,* she is expected to seamlessly spend fifty hours separated from this child!? Be kind and empathetic; this is a lot.

2. **Jump in and help.** There are endless ways: wash her pump parts, pack her lunch, take an extra night shift, or be a safe, judgment-free sounding board.

3. **Educate yourself.** The body undergoes tremendous changes during pregnancy and the postpartum period. Spend some time educating yourself about mothers' perspectives as they transition back to work. This will buttress empathy toward your partner.

4. **Be patient if her libido has not returned.** It *will* return with rest, recovery, and support. Do not pressure her. She will let you know when her libido is back.

5. **If you need professional support, do not wait.** Did you know that one in every ten dads experience a perinatal mood or anxiety disorder? If you suspect that you are experiencing a mood or anxiety disorder, seek professional help. Postpartum.net has a wealth of resources and can connect you with local support.

6. **Remind your partner that *she is enough*.** She will likely need many reminders that she is enough. Women have been socialized to believe they *must* do it all and do so flawlessly. *And,* if they fall short of this toxic fantasy, they have done something wrong. Guilt can overflow when she realizes the impossibility of this fantasy. Remind her that *she is enough*.

7. **Encourage self-health.** Whether it be encouraging her to replenish her body with healthy foods or reconnect with a loved one, encourage her to focus on her eight dimensions of wellness.

8. **Strengthen trust.** Show up and follow through. If you say you will take the night shift, *take the night shift* and do so with a positive, supportive attitude.

MOM FRIENDS, THE OLD AND THE NEW

Try, for just a moment, imagining your life without one of your dearest friends. How do you feel? When I tried this exercise for the first time, my heart literally hurt. We need each other, more than ever, during this season of life. I say this with a qualifier. Our friendships will *never* be the same. Transitioning to employed motherhood changes you at the cellular level; it forces us to grow in ways that we could never fathom as possible. With this growth, our friendships consequently evolve. Some will fade, some will deepen, and others will take a temporary backseat. In the coming sections we will collaboratively explore ways to navigate (1) maintaining and evolving *old* friendships and (2) establishing and nourishing *new* friendships.

Maintaining and Evolving Old Friendships

The fact is, after a major life event, old friendships are going to evolve. This is a healthy, normal process. Perhaps some of these friendships are longstanding and meaningful. Perhaps others are simply comfortable and familiar but not necessarily bringing you joy at this stage of life. Or worse, this is a friendship that has caused undue stress and you would be *relieved* for it to dissolve.

Here are some recommendations for maintaining old friendships:

1. Ask yourself, **"Is the juice worth the squeeze?"** Meaning, is this a friendship you *want* to maintain in this next season of your life or worth maintaining for future seasons. If yes, read on.

2. **Communicate.** If you have not spoken to this person since you've given birth, explain *why*. Maybe you are exhausted or completely immersed in the land of new motherhood. Let them know that you are not intentionally neglecting them and that you care about the friendship. If there is an elephant in the room, *name it*. The elephant will become visible at some point, so you might as well communicate about it now and in a productive, healthy way. A common challenge is navigating a friendship in which the other is struggling with infertility. I recommend clearing the air and making space for those thoughts and feelings. *Hear* one another and offer validation and empathy. This does not have to be an emotional wedge but can create a closer bond.

3. **Intersect your two worlds.** When you are up to it, begin intersecting your friendship and your world as a mother. These relationships do *not* have to compete but can intersect. I vividly remember my first *moms' night out*. I was anxious, ecstatic, and full of adrenaline! When my girlfriend arrived, I gladly handed her the baby as I rushed to finish my makeup. I will never forget the moment of hearing the sounds of my daughter cooing at my girlfriend's ridiculous baby voice! Most importantly, I will never forget the way I *felt* as I paused, realizing that two of my most important relationships were creating their own relationship. It did not have to feel binary; it could feel *gray*. Gray in that these two very different relationships and worlds were finally coming together to create a beautiful tapestry.

How to handle a friendship that is increasingly strained:

1. **Determine if this is a friendship worth fighting for.** In this season of life defined by constant demands, managing relational conflict is the last item on your to-do list. It is important to determine if this friendship is worth the energy output. If not, determine if you need to make a clean break or if you want to gently let it fizzle out or take a back seat for an undetermined amount of time.

2. **Adjust expectations.** If a friendship continues to be ruled by outdated expectations – from either your end or theirs – lower them. This misalignment can often happen with your childless friends. There is *no* possible way to explain to someone without children what this transition is like. Perhaps they don't check in on you as much as you need, perhaps they think you can pick up with your old social habits, as if nothing had changed. They may not be able to empathize when you are on day seven of a teething baby while managing a full-time job. If this is a friendship that's worth the effort, the best thing to do is dust off those "I-Feel" statements and give them a go.

3. **Be mindful of the grief process.** Grieving what once was is a healthy, normal process. A helpful conceptualization of your emotional process surrounding the grief of a friendship is Kübler-Ross' Stages of Grief model, which identifies five stages of grief: denial, anger, bargaining, depression, and acceptance. Because this process is non-linear, it is normal to jump around between the stages.

Establishing and Nourishing New Friendships

Establishing and nourishing new friendships, a period when time is truly a limited resource, requires intentionality to the enth degree. When you and your friends find yourselves in alignment, you feel a connection and share a give-and-take – something employed mothers deserve more of. Here are some helpful factors to consider when establishing and nourishing new friendships.

1. **Compatibility.** No friendship is a perfect match, but some basic compatibilities can make or break the friendship. Areas of compatibility include *parenting style*, *age of child(ren)*, *temperament of mother/child(ren)*, and *logistics* such as scheduling and availability.

2. **Check comparisons.** Comparison is the thief of joy and the grass is not always greener. Check those comparisons as soon as they surface. Resist the urge to compare yourself to the other mom or your child to her child(ren). We all have strengths and weaknesses, and our diversity makes us stronger. What you probably do not realize is that despite the other mom *having it all together*, she is suffering in ways you could never imagine.

3. **Boundaries.** Set healthy boundaries from the get-go and observe if those boundaries are respected by the other person. In friendships, especially in this busy and exhausting season, boundaries not only protect us and the other person, but also the relationship. If you are too exhausted to make it to the playdate and need to cancel, how does the other person respond? Are they supportive and understanding? These are good questions to ask yourself as you navigate the development of friendships.

4. **Willingness for vulnerability.** The last thing employed mothers need is a friend who talks all about the perfections of employed motherhood. Be *real*. Be *vulnerable*. Offer a safe space for vulnerability. Resist judgments, projections, or the temptation to perpetuate the toxic expectations of employed mothers to pretend that everything is unicorns and rainbows. Look at someone's wiliness for vulnerability as a barometer for assessing if this is a friendship you want to nourish.

Ways to Meet Moms

Smartphone Apps like Peanuts & Hello Mamas

Stroller Strides

Facebook Groups

Join a local Moms Group

Online Communities

PARENTS AND IN-LAWS

The parenting demands faced by your parents' and in-laws' generation is incomparable to the demands of today's parenting, especially those faced by employed mothers. It is *impossible* for your parents or in-laws to fathom what you are experiencing. Expecting them to fully understand is an unfair expectation, as much as we want them to mindread and feel what we feel. What *is* a healthy expectation is that they check-in, offer support, and refrain from making judgments. If I had a nickel, just a nickel, for every employed mother who told me they had received some form of passive aggressive remarks or social media tags from their parent or in-law, I would be one rich mama. Remember, though, as insulting and offensive as unsolicited or unhelpful solicited advice can be, the parent or in-law giving such is likely projecting their *own* stuff onto you. This has nothing to do with you and everything to do with them.

Here are some tricks for managing unsolicited comments for parents or in-laws:

1. **Selectively respond.** Identify one aspect of what your parent or in-law is saying and agree with that *one* piece.

2. **Passively respond.** Passively respond then change the subject. "Huh, okay." "Interesting thought." *Or* simply nod and keep on moving.

3. **Topic avoidance.** Avoid topics that you know are triggering. For example, if your mother-in-law repeatedly makes passive aggressive comments about your co-sleeping or nursing habits, steer clear of these subjects when possible.

4. **Utilize a mediator (AKA your partner).** If you or your partner have used multiple strategies with little or no success, have your partner set clear and firm boundaries. "Dad, we love you, but we need to leave by 7 p.m. in order to start our son's bedtime routine."

5. **Knowledge is power.** You are no doubt an expert when it comes to your baby's (and your own) needs. You have read articles, consulted with your pediatrician, and know a thing or two from all of those late-night Dr. Google searches. Go ahead – unapologetically – and quote the articles. *Or,* better yet, your pediatrician!

When your parents or in-laws are caregivers

While interviewing employed mothers for this book, the topic of parents and in-laws caring for your child evoked a wide range of advice. I am not sure even just two moms gave the same piece of advice. This presents a challenge in constructing a general guide for navigating this topic as it is multifactorial and complex. What I compiled, though, are highlights from employed mothers on this topic. Take what you need, leave what you don't!

Advice from employed mothers on the topic of parents and in-laws stepping into a childcare role:

- "Openly communicate the needs of your child, and on the regular."

- "Be mindful to provide opportunities for them to take off the childcare hat and just be grandparents, especially if they are providing full-time care."

- "Consider goodness-of-fit and compatibility if you are going have another part-time childcare provider. My parents refused to get on board with the other care-giver's schedule and approach. It felt like a constant battle."

- "It made all the difference when I became more intentional and offered acknowledgement and appreciation."

- "I will *never* ask my parents to provide any form of consistent childcare. This would create too much role confusion for *everyone!*"

- "If you are worried about your parent's physical limitations, ask what they need. I worried for so long and when I finally told my mom I was worried about her slipping, we found some really great house slippers which alleviated a lot of angst."

SARAH WILCOX DOULA, CLD CPD EPI-DOULA CLSE

Demystifying Hiring a Postpartum Doula

Sarah Wilcox practices in the southwestern region of the United States as a Certified Doula. She is also a proud mother to four children. Throughout my interview with Sarah, she circled back to the Ancient Greek meaning of *doula,* servant. Sarah highlights that doulas come into the lives of postpartum families to *serve,* whatever that looks like. Services are focused on the needs of the family and *flexible*, ranging from education on workplace rights, figuring out how to pack a pumping bag for your first day back to work, or acting as a safe listening ear after a rough night. "Becky," she told me, "You do not have to do it all on your own. We should not have to stretch ourselves so thin. You are *not* weak if you ask for help."

Sarah demystifies the process of hiring a doula during this season of life, reminding moms that services are custom-tailored to the needs of the family. She encourages moms to reconstruct a contract if needs change. For example, many moms realize that during the first few weeks back to work they need more hours than initially contracted. "Just ask. Most of the time we can figure out something that works for everyone." Sarah often hears from prospective clients that the cost is daunting, especially on top of the financial burden accompanying a newborn, when it does not need to be. Payment plans can be worked out. Trading services is also not unheard of.

For mothers with other children, Sarah recommends hiring a sibling doula. These specialized doulas can provide invaluable services to older siblings. Sibling doulas can provide caretaking, educate siblings in developmentally appropriate ways, and serve in whatever capacity they are needed.

Sarah hired a postpartum doula following the birth of her fourth child. She was finishing her degree (akin to full-time employment) and was a single mother, no easy feat. This was an aha moment for her, as receiving the services from her cherished doula blossomed into a fuller appreciation for doulas. Her doula provided valuable information for her pumping rights at the university she attended and ways to healthily manage full-time school, a newborn, and three other children.

PAID SUPPORTS

Want a foolproof recipe for burnout? Believe you have to do it all – and then try to do it. I'll say it again: employed motherhood is a *lot* of work. You'll have to ask for help – but you'll also have to accept it. Sure, your best friend can recommend her cleaner, but if you just jot down her contact info and never make the first phone call, your house won't actually get any cleaner. There's no prize awarded for the mom who "does it all." The "prize" comes when we make the mindset adjustment that allows us to outsource without guilt. *Many* employed moms have chosen to pay for support as they realize that *doing it all* is unsustainable – by any degree.

Barriers to Accessing Paid Support

I want you to name all of the lies you are telling yourself. How are these lies creating a barrier to paying for support? As I interviewed employed mothers, some phrases I heard were:

Lie 1: "Somehow my mother managed to raise five children, keep a full-time job, *and* our house was always clean!" Comparison is the thief of all joy, and it is *not* fair to compare generations that are apples and oranges. Your mom indubitably struggled raising five children, and what you saw externally was the mask that she wore. Instead of perpetually wearing this "keep it together" mask, how about we all take it off, acknowledge the impossibility of *doing it all*, and go ahead and outsource some support.

Lie 2: "I can't afford to outsource." My rebuttal to this lie? You cannot *not* afford to outsource. Burning from both ends comes with a cost, whether via self-medicating through shopping, substances, eating, or any other form of self-destructive behavior. Sit down with your budget and allocate money in other areas to make room for outsourcing. Sure, $20/week in grocery delivery adds up, but grocery shopping under stress will easily add $20 to that shopping cart.

Lie 3: "Every employed mom has to juggle a *million* things. I should too. I just need to get more efficient." You can be efficient down to the millisecond, but there is simply not enough time in the day to do all of the things that we need to do. Motherhood is insatiable! Gently remind yourself that you are *enough* and give yourself permission to access paid support.

Some kinds of paid support employed mothers have found helpful:

1. **Postpartum Doula.** A postpartum doula wears multiple hats: educator, counselor, coach, advocate, housekeeper, and beyond. Instead of focusing solely on the baby, a postpartum doula focuses on the mother and baby as well as the family as a whole. Postpartum doulas tailor their services so what they provide is unique to your needs. Some services include assistance with lactation, postpartum education and support, strategies for

oothing an infant, light housekeeping, sibling support, meal preparation, and connection
o local and community resources. Some hospitals provide low-cost doula services by
onnecting doulas-in-training with families.

Newborn Care Specialist (NCS). Newborn care specialists focus solely on the baby.
ome responsibilities include general care, sleep training, bathing, diapering, sanitation of
ump parts and bottles, feeding, overnight care, nursery organization, and detection of
medical issues.

Physical Therapist. Postpartum physical therapy can provide relief and recovery from
gamut of conditions ranging from pain, diastasis recti, pelvic floor damage, mobility, and
eyond. When I returned to work, I was already struggling with lower back pain. Since I
at for long stretches of my day, not to mention pumping several times, the pain magnified
vith time. Physical therapy relieved pain and taught me stretches I could complete at home
nd throughout my workday. Many insurance plans cover physical therapists; you should
e able to use your tax-free Health Savings Account funds toward physical therapy as well.

Licensed Mental Health Professional (Perinatal Specialist – PMH-C). Therapists
re invaluable when it comes to your mental, emotional, and relational health. If you even
uspect that you might be suffering from a postpartum mood or anxiety disorder, consult
vith a professional. I recommend finding a provider who has specialized perinatal training
ike a certified perinatal mental health professional, also referred to as a PMH-C. *Or,* if you
imply need a safe sounding board to support you in this major life transition, therapists
an also just *listen.* Verbal processing is effective in sorting all of the pieces encompassed
n this transition. Many insurance plans cover mental health services; you should be able
o use your tax-free Health Savings Account funds for counseling as well.

5. **Life Coach.** Life coaches can join with you to identify pragmatic solutions focused on
he *now,* as well as bridge the gap between now and where you want to be. I appreciated the
upport of a life coach as I transitioned my private practice back to a full-time caseload
ifter having my second daughter.

5. **Dieticians.** Dieticians can help you navigate ways to replenish your nutrients through
food with the ultimate goal of recovering from pregnancy and childbirth. Additional
benefits include increasing your energy level, maintaining nutrient-dense milk if you
ire lactating, and integrating foods into your diet to support your brain and hormonal
function. Many insurance plans cover dieticians; you should be able to use your tax-free
Health Savings Account funds to cover appointment costs as well.

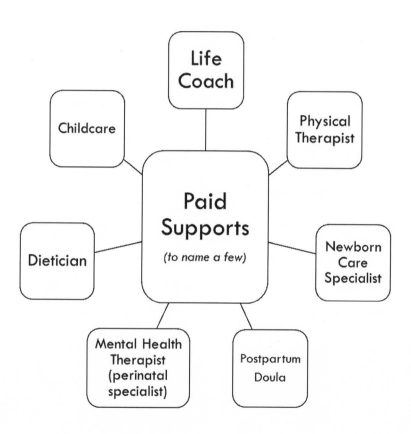

Dearest Employed Mother,

Employed motherhood is not for the faint of heart. We are transforming as a world, creating a script for how all of this works. Or – figuring out how it doesn't work. Not an easy feat. If this is the only section of the book you read, know that you are not alone. There are millions of us. Know that you are fierce. Know that you are capable. Know that you are worthy of support. Mindfully dance through each question mark. This season is temporary. You *will* see the forest through the trees. You have done hard things, and you can continue to do hard things. You have *so* got this.

I would love to hear about your transition to employed motherhood! Contact me on any of my social media platforms.

I am cheering you on, Mama.

Sending you my warmest regards,

Becky

EMPLOYED MOTHERS' CAFETERIA OF RESOURCES

Pick and Choose What You Need

A Better Balance "uses the power of the law to advance justice for workers, so they can care for themselves and their loved ones without jeopardizing their economic security." They have an expert legal team that combats "discrimination against pregnant workers and caregivers and advances supportive policies like paid sick time, paid family and medical leave, fair scheduling, and accessible, quality childcare and eldercare. When we value the work of providing care, which has long been marginalized due to sexism and racism, our communities and our nation are healthier and stronger."

https://www.abetterbalance.org

Devlaux Law AKA MAMATTORNEY is a mom of two who has dedicated her law practice to helping working women.

https://www.themamattorney.com

Fairygodboss has evolved well beyond their original vision to provide a platform for women to review their employers. Additional features now include a social network for women returning to the workforce, job listings, education, and relevant content and resources to support women in the workplace.

https://www.fairygodboss.com

Families & Work Institute is a nonprofit organization dedicated to "providing research for living in today's changing workplace, changing family, and changing community."

https://www.familiesandwork.org

FlexProfessionals matches companies searching for experienced part-time employees with professionals also looking for part-time employment. FlexProfessionals was founded by employed mothers, all experienced businesswomen, who understand first-hand the need for part-time employment.

https://www.flexprofessionalsllc.com/

The International Center for Research on Women advances the rights of women worldwide by conducting pioneering research on gender inequity in order to propose gender-informed solutions to global issues. In 2016, it merged with **Re:Gender**, an international organization focused on economic empowerment that produced meaningful research in the areas of feminism and women in the workplace.

https://www.icrw.org/

The Mom Project connects employed mothers with companies who work toward honoring work-life harmony. One program, MaternityShip, coordinates a temporary employee to support your work during parental leave . The project includes a job matching program for both freelance and full-time opportunities for moms.

https://www.themomproject.com

Moms' Mental Health Matters is an initiative under the umbrella of The National Institute of Child Health and Human Development. "This initiative is designed to educate consumers and health care providers about who is at risk for depression and anxiety during and after pregnancy, the signs of these problems, and how to get help."

https://www.nichd.nih.gov/ncmhep/initiatives/moms-mental-   health-matters/moms

Moms Rising is an "on-the-ground and online grassroots organization of more than a million people who are working to achieve economic security for all moms, women, and families in the United States. MomsRising is working for paid family leave, earned sick days, affordable childcare, and for an end to the wage and hiring discrimination which penalizes so many mothers. MomsRising also advocates for better childhood nutrition, health care for all, toxic free environments, breastfeeding rights so that all children can have a healthy start, and a national budget that reflects the contributions of women and moms."

https://www.momsrising.org

National Partnership for Women & Families' mission is to "improve the lives of women and families by achieving equality for all women." This is a national, non-profit, non-partisan organization that works to change policy and culture.

https://www.nationalpartnership.org/about-us/

Working Momkind is an online community with a mission to "empower, showcase, and support the hard work and talents of moms around the world." Working Momkind also hosts a variety of events which focuses on bringing employed moms together.

https://www.workingmomkind.com

2020 Mom is focuses on closing the gap on maternal mental health, holding the mission to provide all women in the perinatal period access to evidence-based maternal mental healthcare. They focus on policy, advocacy, and training both individuals and professionals.

https://www.2020mom.org/our-work

PODCASTS WORTH HIGHLIGHTING

Women at Work, Harvard Business Review

Recommended episodes:

Season 2, Episode 9, "Your Parental Leave Stories"

Season 3, Episode 3, "The Upside of Working Motherhood"

Season 4, Episode 6, "How to Make Part Time Work for You"

Season 5, Episode 11, "Welcome Back to Remote Work, New Moms"

Season 6, Episode 2, "How Mother WFH are Negotiating What's Normal"

Beyond Burnout, Tracey Marks

Career Mom, Jenny Elliott

Influential Motherhood, Melissa Duncan

The Working Mother's Mentor, Julie Finn

APPENDICES

Appendix A

Before we dig in, let's highlight you.

First, grab something to write with. Below, write down strengths, positive qualities, the personality traits that you want to celebrate, etc.

1. _____

2. _____

3. _____

4. _____

5. _____

6. _____

7. _____

8. _____

9. _____

10. _____

You existed before you became a mother and that person still matters. It is okay to make room for her. When you experience negative self-talk, remember this list and use it as evidence of all of your strengths. You are enough, just as you are.

Appendix B

Write down three thoughts surrounding your transition back to work:

1.

_____

_____

_____

2.

_____

_____

_____

3.

_____

_____

_____

Write down three feelings (and what's *behind* those feelings) surrounding your transition back to work:

1.

2.

3.

Appendix C

Here is the format for an I-Feel statement:

I feel [insert emotion] when [insert situation or thoughts].

For example:

-Feel Statement: I felt ecstatic seeing Julie, my co-worker, at my first day back. I forgot how stimulating our conversations are and it feels so good to be around adults again!

Practice below:

I feel _____ when _____

I feel _____ when _____

I feel _____ when _____

Appendix D

Empathic response to an *I-FEEL* statement:

_____

_____

_____

Empathic response to an *I-FEEL* statement:

_____

_____

_____

Empathic response to an *I-FEEL* statement:

_____

_____

_____

Empathic response to an *I-FEEL* statement:

_____

_____

_____

Affirmations:

1.

_____

_____

_____

2.

_____

_____

_____

3.

_____

_____

_____

Thoughts:

1.

2.

3.

Feelings:

1.

_____

_____

_____

2.

_____

_____

_____

3.

_____

_____

_____

Appendix E

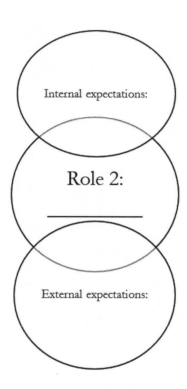

How might internal/external expectations within this role interfere with your new role as a working mother?

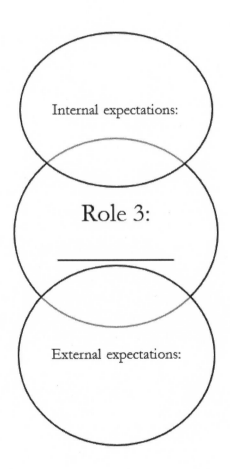

Internal expectations:

Role 3:

_____

External expectations:

How might internal/external expectations within this role interfere with your new role as a working mother?

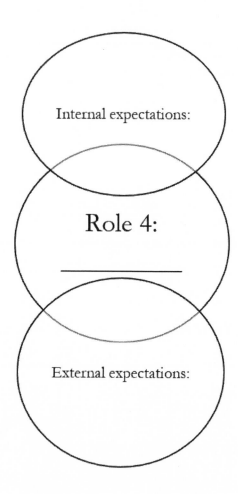

How might internal/external expectations within this role interfere with your new role as a working mother?

Appendix F

What are three short-term financial benefits to remaining in the workforce?

1.

_____

_____

_____

2.

_____

_____

_____

3.

_____

_____

_____

What are three long-term financial benefits to remaining in the workforce?

1.

_____

_____

_____

2.

_____

_____

_____

3.

_____

_____

_____

Appendix G

What went well?

_____

_____

_____

_____

_____

_____

_____

_____

What could have gone better?

_____

_____

_____

_____

_____

_____

_____

Appendix H

Macro Protections

Parental leave:

1.

_____

_____

_____

2.

_____

_____

_____

3.

_____

_____

_____

Pregnancy-related disability (if applicable):

1.

_____

_____

_____

2.

_____

_____

_____

3.

_____

_____

Pumping in the workplace:

1.

_____

_____

_____

2.

_____

_____

_____

3.

_____

_____

_____

Micro Protections

Parental leave:

1.

_____

_____

_____

2.

_____

_____

_____

3.

_____

_____

_____

Pregnancy-related disability (if applicable):

1.

_____

_____

_____

2.

_____

_____

_____

3.

_____

_____

_____

Pumping in the workplace:

1.

_____

_____

_____

2.

_____

_____

_____

3.

_____

_____

_____

Appendix I

Here is an exercise to try:

Place colleagues in each of the following categories:

Casual colleagues

_____

_____

_____

Collaborative colleagues

_____

_____

_____

Intimate colleagues

_____

_____

_____

from here, would you like anyone from the casual category to move to the social or intimate category? Or – would it be better for your health to move someone from the intimate category to social or casual? How can you make that happen? Have fun with this visual and identify who you want where! The next step is nourishing those relationships accordingly. *Derived from interpersonal Psychotherapy Theory (IPT).*[32]

Casual colleagues

_____

_____

_____

Collaborative colleagues

_____

_____

_____

Intimate colleagues

_____

_____

_____

32   Markowitz, J. C., & Weissman, M. M. (2004). Interpersonal psychotherapy: Principles and applications. *World Psychiatry: Official Journal of the World Psychiatric Association (WPA)*, 3(3), 136–139. https://www.ncbi.nlm. nih.gov/pubmed/16633477

Made in the USA
Middletown, DE
21 June 2023

32416951R00128